THE EMBROIDERER'S WORK

THE EMBROIDERER'S WORKBOOK

Jan Messent

St. Martin's Press, New York

ISBN 0–312–02121–6

First published in Great Britain by B. T. Batsford Ltd, 1988

First U.S. Edition, 1989
10 9 8 7 6 5 4 3 2 1

Typeset by Tek-Art Ltd, Kent

Contents

Acknowledgements

Special thanks to Rachel Wright of Batsford who gave me the opportunity to present my ideas in technicolour, for a change! Also to Valerie Campbell-Harding, my special thanks for her invaluable advice on the structure and contents of the book. Mary Holden and Victoria Macleod most generously made their City and Guilds embroideries (and ideas) available to me; to them and to their respective tutors I offer my grateful thanks. The photograph which appears as fig. 42 was taken by John Hetherington, a student friend of my husband, who could not be traced for permission to use it, but to whom I offer apologies, and thanks.

Except for that which is otherwise credited, all the work was done by myself, much of it especially for this book.

Introduction

This book aims to fulfil two main purposes. The first is to attempt to take the place of tutor to all those enthusiastic embroiderers who find, for various reasons, that they are unable to attend classes. Many of us have been in this situation, knowing that wonderful things are happening in the world of embroidery and being destined never to discover what they are or how they are created; families, illnesses and distances all put up obstacles we find hard to overcome, and books full of beautiful embroideries almost convince us that we are being overtaken on all sides by brilliant and gifted people. Not so; determination to commandeer some time of our own, a push or two in the right direction from the suggestions in this book, and we shall be well on the way to joining our embroidering sisters on equal terms.

The second purpose of the book is to persuade students of embroidery (with or without tutors) that experiments are vital to a better understanding of the craft, and that exercises *for their own sake* are as necessary to embroiderers as they are to writers, artists and musicians. Imagine a writer who never learnt any grammar, an artist who never practised figure-drawing or a musician who never played any scales! Emphasis has been placed on the need to keep a notebook or file of exercises as a reference for the future, and this is important not only to City and Guilds students but to all who take their embroidery seriously enough to want to improve. This notebook can be an attractive acquisition, as many of my 'notebook-page' illustrations seek to show, and should contain all the aids to discovery which you have made, and without which all your ideas would have remained unborn.

I sincerely hope that all who use this book and find it useful will derive as much pleasure from it as I have done while working on its contents.

1 'Warrior's Head'. A life-sized
three-dimensional head which has
now been adapted as a table
ornament with a fitted box
underneath the beard and hair. The
helmet is a colourful log-cabin
patchwork, and the face and hair
are dark brown felt, leather and
wool. (Photo: V.A. Campbell-
Harding)

1 Pattern

The vocabulary of pattern

Expressed quite simply, a pattern is composed of units which are repeated enough times within a design to make this repetition a prominent or noticeable feature. It does not matter whether the units are repeated at random or in a formal arrangement, whether they are all the same size or varied; the important element is the shape. Below is a list of words used in connection with pattern.

Unit: the repeating element in a pattern.
Motif: the dominant element, or subject, which will be repeated.
Interval: the area, or space, between recurring elements; the distance between.
Positive space: the shape/space to which you are giving major prominence.
Negative space: the shape left void, or undecorated between positive shapes. (These two can change places.)
Counterchange: this happens when the negative and positive shapes change roles, i.e. you give the more prominent role to the negative shape, and then change back again further on in the pattern.
Network: lines (straight or wavy) which are laid to form the basis of the grid. They may or may not become part of the pattern.
Grid: the system of shapes into which the pattern is to be set, e.g. squares, hexagons, etc.
Repeat: the addition of one complete unit, exactly like the others, appropriately placed on the grid.
Random/irregular pattern: repeats which do not fit into a formal grid, e.g. soap bubbles, pebbles.
Regular/formal pattern: repeats arranged in an organized way, e.g. bricks and tiles, knitted fabrics.
Border pattern: one made from repeats arranged vertically or horizontally. Corners are designed using a mirror.
Symmetrical: a design, or motif, which is a mirror image of itself from a central line (vertical or horizontal). The opposite of this is known as 'asymmetry' and the design as 'asymmetrical'.

Other words used in connection with pattern-making are : vertical, horizontal, perpendicular, diagonal and mirror image, and need no explanantion.
Note: a *rectangle* is a four-sided figure in which the *two opposite sides* are parallel and of the same length. A *square* also fits this description, as all its sides are the same length.

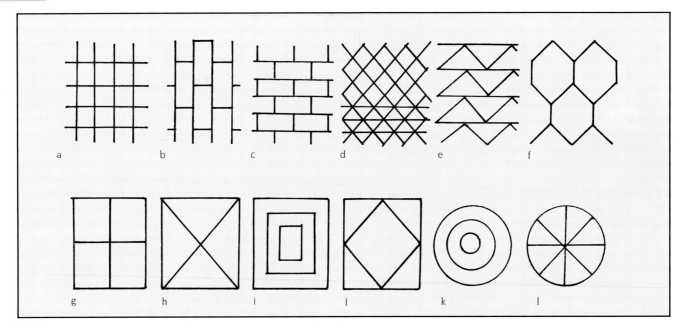

2 *Some commonly used grids for pattern-making. Top line: (a) square, (b) half-drop, (c) brick, (d) diamond/triangle, (e) pointed scale and (f) hexagon. Second line: dividing the square, with (g) squares, (h) diagonals, (i) smaller squares, (j) crossed corners; dividing the circle with (k) concentric rings and (l) radial lines.*

Experiments in formal arrangement

The shapes seen at the top of the opposite page fit together with repeats of their own kind and are commonly used as 'building blocks' to make grids. There are many ways to make all-over patterns and borders, some of which are:

1 experimenting to find ways of arranging motifs inside shapes;
2 finding ways of arranging and rearranging the shapes;
3 trying out combinations of grids, e.g. squares inside circles, triangles inside squares;
4 using shading to place the emphasis on different parts of the motif, and its space inside the shape (counterchange).

● Collect material illustrating all aspects of pattern, and organize it to show formal and random patterns, those from nature, man-made sources, coloured, mono-chrome, etc. Keep your own sketches and photographs with this material too for future reference. Build up a file.

● The examples opposite show the different effects created by outlines and by changing the tone in the background and on the motif. Do this in your experiments, as each style creates a different impression. It may also suggest different techniques for embroidery.

● Compose border patterns using any of the shapes shown here. Choose one of the following subjects: a letter of the alphabet, a flower, a snail, a shell, a footprint. To turn a corner, use a straight-sided handmirror (one without a frame): place one edge on the pattern and hold the mirror vertically and at right-angles to the paper. Now move it on the pattern until a corner arrangement appears in the mirror, and then adjust it until you find a suitable pattern which can be copied into the corner of your design.

● Try out one unit in a multiple arrangement like the ones seen in 3. Tracing paper is useful for this exercise as the motif can be traced several times from the original, then placed in different positions, allowing you to see the effects before you decide on a final placing.

3

Geometric pattern

Many embroiderers express themselves solely in the use of geometric pattern, not because they are unable to draw, but because they find the interrelationships of formal shapes a perfect way of exploiting fabrics, colours, textures and patterns. All techniques lend themselves to geometric constructions and all stitches make patterns. Traditional techniques such as pulled work, hardanger and needle-weaving can be introduced alongside machine embroidery and patchwork to create patterns of combined textures and effects.

Experiments

- Collect samples of paper bags, wrapping paper, wallpaper and magazine cuttings which are printed with geometric patterns, also pieces of fabric with stripes, dots, checks, etc. and other formal patterns of a geometric nature.
- Cut patterned paper into smallish squares, depending on the scale, and reassemble them to form a different pattern. Stick these down in your notebook. You may wish to leave some spaces in your pattern by removing some pieces altogether.
- Cut striped paper into strips of different widths and rearrange them; also *weave* them to make a rectangle of different colours, and stick them in place. The idea is not to see this only as a piece of fabric patchwork, but to use the result as the basis of, for instance (*i*) a piece of fine canvas work; (*ii*) any stitchery which resembles the original as closely as possible; (*iii*) an exercise in tonal values using blackwork or any stitch in tones of one colour.
- Using striped paper, mark out an equilateral triangle with sides of about 10 cm (4 in.) and cut this up into about 16 small equal triangles. Now reassemble these to form the large triangle with the stripes going in different directions. Stick these in position, and add embellishments such as braid or cord if you feel they are needed.

- Using smallish pieces of striped, checked or other patterned fabrics, make pleats, pin-tucks and folds across the pattern to see what effects are produced. Any frayed edges can be used as part of the design. (Striped pillow ticking is useful for this exercise.) Pin or stick these in place and add matching threads for extra effect or emphasis. Try adding small checks on top of large ones, and small stripes on top of wide stripes.
- Paper-cutting is a childhood activity which we may have forgotten about, but is a useful way of constructing designs for embroidery. Use patterned paper, folded into a rectangle or into vertical folds (concertina) and snip small bits from the edges with sharp scissors. Make circular patterns (like doilies) from colourful magazine pages and place them over plain paper (when cut) to show a different colour beneath, or use gold or silver paper as the bottom layer. If you choose a colour for the bottom layer which echoes one of those in the cut piece, you may find that part of the pattern disappears, as it fuses with its counterpart below, thus creating another interesting effect which may be copied in stitchery.

4 (*a*) *Striped paper bag cut into strips then woven, overlaid with narrow blue ribbon.* (*b*) *Striped paper bag cut into large triangle then into sixteen small ones, rearranged and stuck down.* (*c*) *The largest pattern underneath is folded and cut coloured wrapping paper. On top of this in the top corner is a sample of lettering, and in the lower corner another folded and cut pattern from a magazine page. Overlaid, these patterns merge to produce an interesting effect.* (*d*) *Two different striped wrapping papers cut into 2-centimetre squares and rearranged to form one large square, then decorated with sequin waste, braids, gold cord and net.* (*e*) *Embroidered sample worked in satin stitch on a striped fabric. The colours of the stripes become more pronounced where they converge with the design. The outer square is of satin stitch worked over card, and the central one is of fabric-covered card.* (*f*) *Striped fabric, extra pieces cut into narrow strips of varying widths then laid over the background so that the stripes are broken. Extra cords of metallic yarn and squares of gold mesh added.* (*g: bottom row*) *Cuttings from magazines in the same geometric theme, more folded paper patterns, the little figures made of coloured-pencil stripes on white paper.*

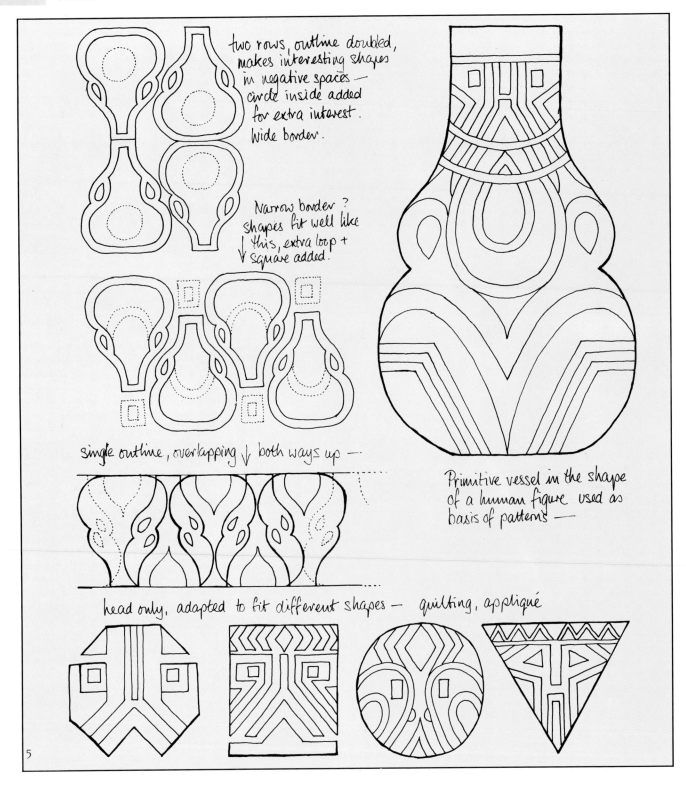

two rows, outline doubled, makes interesting shapes in negative spaces — circle inside added for extra interest. Wide border.

Narrow border? shapes fit well like this, extra loop + square added!

single outline, overlapping ↓ both ways up —

Primitive vessel in the shape of a human figure used as basis of patterns —

head only, adapted to fit different shapes — quilting, appliqué

5

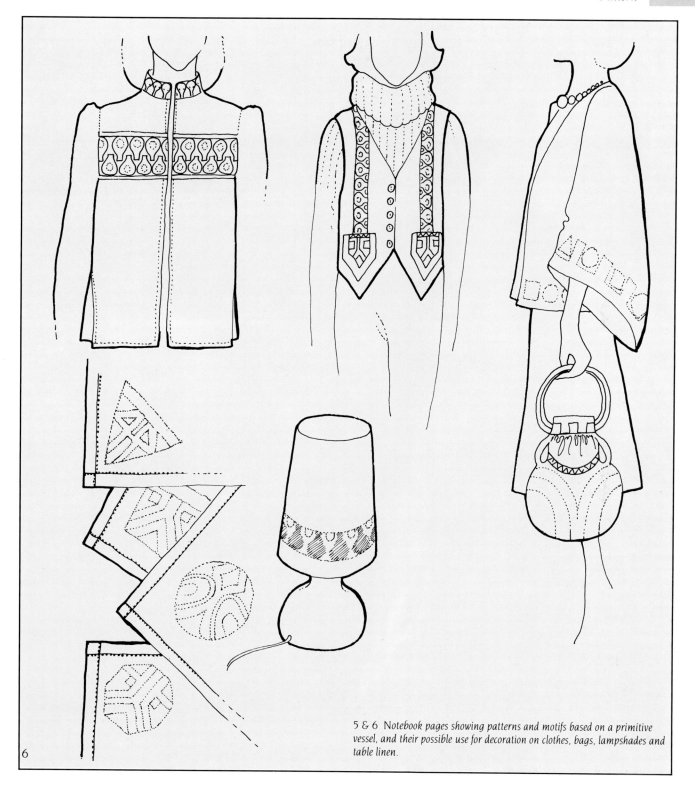

5 & 6 Notebook pages showing patterns and motifs based on a primitive vessel, and their possible use for decoration on clothes, bags, lampshades and table linen.

6

7

Informal pattern

If you examine the examples shown here (7), you will see that all of them contain the essential element of pattern – that is, a repeating element. Some have repeating curved or straight lines, others have squares or triangles, and some have a mixture of these. In each case, though, another unrelated motif has been introduced – unrelated *visually*, that is. The only exception is the M (top left) which grows quite happily from its surrounding geometric shapes. The other motifs, the head, shirt, cat and lettering, are simply interesting shapes which have been super-imposed on (or placed in between) the pattern elements, to break them up into smaller areas. In the case of the three designs with words, the words were chosen to fit into the pattern shapes, rather than the other way round. Looking hard at the bare lines of pattern and allowing it to suggest a meaning is one way of finding words which seem to fit. In the case of the shirt over the triangle, a very loose and wavy shape was required to relieve the symmetry of the triangles and circle.

Try these ideas with basic pattern grids inside a square, then counterchange the tones to make a balanced design. Don't use colour at first: concentrate on shapes, lines and tonal values, and on an overall balance of ideas.

The order is as follows:

1 Draw a 7.5 cm (3 in.) square.
2 Draw lines across it, straight or wavy, or shaped like triangles and circles. Use any of the basic grid shapes you see here.
3 Now think of an entirely unrelated shape such as a fish, a teapot, a capital letter, a bird, a hand, or words, and *either* draw one of these over the top of your grid lines (as seen top right) or draw it between the lines (as seen centre left). You must make this extra shape big enough to fill the space. Look at the examples here as a guide.
4 Now add details to make the design more interesting: more areas of pattern, shading or texture, building up in this way until the design balances. Leave some areas of plain white as well as the detailed parts, otherwise your design may begin to look fussy and over-crowded.
5 Now think about embroidery. Would any of your ideas adapt to a particular technique? Appliqué, pulled thread, blackwork, stitchery or patchwork? If so, draw the idea out again, this time with any alterations you need to make it work in your chosen technique. Use a suggestion of colour too (either paint or coloured pencils), but keep to the *same tones* as your original. This may then be kept in your notebook until you need it, or you may wish to go straight on to the embroidery.

8 *Tyre tracks in mud.* (Photo: Jan Messent)

Projects

Tyre patterns

For anyone who prefers the geometric type of pattern, there is a rich source of inspiration to be found in tyres. Tracks can be seen quite clearly in muddy fields, sometimes filled with water or ice, or mixed in with grass and flowers. Tyre patterns can also be found in advertisements and in car magazines. They can be used either as border patterns or extended sideways for a more widthways arrangement.

1 Try interpretations in monochrome, monotone and in full colour.
2 Simplify or add to the pattern, and experiment with fabric alone as well as with stitchery.
3 Use the patterns as decoration on articles as well as the subjects of panels which might have titles such as 'Making Tracks', 'Track Record', 'Back Track', 'Spare Tyre' or 'Tread Gently'. Thinking along these lines may help to suggest a way in which tyre patterns could feature as an important element in a design, rather than simply as a pattern exercise.

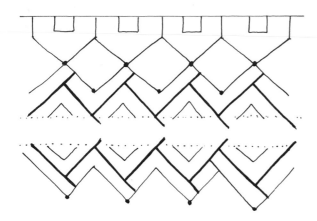

9 *Tyre patterns.*

4 Make this a full-scale project lasting several weeks (or even months) while you collect cuttings and other resource material in the shape of drawings and photographs of mud-tracks and of stacks of tyres seen in scrapyards. The ingenuity of some of these patterns is quite remarkable. You can see a very small sample of them here, though cycle tyres are different widths, and tractor and lorry tyres also.

5 Adapt some of your ideas to various embroidery techniques, such as canvas work (needlepoint) and other counted-thread methods. Also use patchwork and appliqué, cutwork and quilting.

Variegated leaves

This subject has the advantage of being adaptable to both the formal and informal layout, and also brings with it a colour-scheme which may or may not be kept to. The patterns of, and on, the leaves is the important aspect of the project; the colours are of secondary importance. The patterns on the leaves may be suggested instead by tonal changes in a monochrome scheme, or by different *textures* in a monotone scheme, such as in cutwork or pulled thread. You will also see in the photograph that the volume of leaves makes its own pattern.

Make simplified drawings, like the ones shown here, and use pale paint or coloured pencils to reproduce the effect of the variegated patterns. Don't use fibre pens for this, as they are too harsh and unsympathetic. Try quilting the pattern on some small sample pieces; shadow quilting is also a good way of capturing the soft and gentle colours found in leaves. Use paint on some parts of the design (see page 32) and try to retain the delicate effect of random pattern which can be seen in the photograph. Collect ideas from garden catalogues and gardening magazines for your notebook, and keep all these together for reference, along with your experiments. Design a small purse or bag which makes use of one of your designs.

10 *Patterns of coleus leaves.* (Photo: Jan Messent)

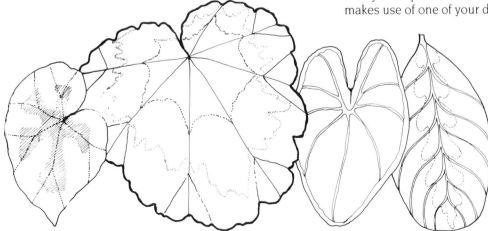

11 *Variegated leaf patterns.*

12 An experiment by Mary Holden combining log-cabin patchwork and canvas work. Each square measures 16.5 cm (6½ in.), being a fabric-covered frame enclosing a combination of vibrant reds, blues, greens and black. The more usual reverse side of the patchwork is now the right side, allowing the frayed edges to become a feature of the design. Each one encloses a tiny square of fine canvas, each one a different pattern, the colours echoing those of the fabrics and the fragments of machine embroidery on them.

2
Colour

The basic vocabulary of colour

Primary colours: there are three: red, blue and yellow, indicated by a square on the edge of the colour-wheel.
Secondary colours: these are made by mixing together any two primaries, and are marked by triangles.
Tertiary colours: these are made by combining any primary with any secondary and are the unmarked ones on the colour-wheel, though many other variations are possible. If all three primaries are mixed together, the result is grey.
Hue: this is the pure colour with nothing added to make it lighter or darker.
Tint: any hue with the addition of white to make it paler. These are shown on the outer edge of the colour-wheel.
Shade: this is the hue with the addition of black (or another dark colour) to make it darker. Shades are shown on the inside of the colour-wheel. *Note*: there are countless variations of tints and shades depending on how much of each colour is added.
Tone: how light or dark a colour is. We often use the word 'shade' to describe it, but this is not strictly correct. All hues, tints and shades are tones of colour in relation to black and white, for example, a red-violet is dark in tone, and a yellow-green is light. The tonal values of the hues, tints and shades of some colours are easy to assess, but to assess the tonal values of colours *in relation to each other* is more difficult and needs practice.
Scheme: a chosen combination of colours.

Some types of scheme are described below:

Complementary: colours which lie opposite, or approximately opposite, to each other on the colour-wheel. Primary colours are complementary to their opposite secondaries, and tertiaries are always complementary to their opposite tertiaries. Complementary colours provide the greatest amount of contrast.
Analogous (adjacent, similar): colours plus their tints and shades which lie next to each other on the colour-wheel.

The chosen colours can range from two to six segments, that is, up to one-third of the colour-wheel.
Monochromatic: a scheme of one colour only, plus its tints and shades.
Triadic: three colours placed at equal distances apart on the colour-wheel.
Chroma: this word is used to describe the amount of pure colour. A colour with a high chroma may, for example, be bright yellow, while one with a low chroma (that is, with a low proportion of the pure hue) may be grey/blue.
Neutral: colours of low chroma, including all the greys, white, black and so-called 'dull' colours, though to name them so is not to recognize their true value in colour-schemes.
Warm colours: used to describe colours such as red, orange and yellow, or colours containing a high proportion of these.
Cool colours: thought to be blues and greens and associated colours, while violet and yellow take their warmth or coolness from the colours which surround them.
Advance and recede: colours which appear to 'come forward' (i.e. attract more instant attention) when placed with other colours are said to *advance*, while those which are less bright are said to *recede* and give an impression of distance. Advancing colours are red, orange and yellow, and receding colours are violet and blue. Painters use this theory to good effect in their use of violet-blues for distances.
Harmony: a scheme of colours which balances, whether it is analogous or complementary. Usually the colours used in a harmonious scheme are very much alike in character, and do nothing to 'alarm' or make one feel uncomfortable.
Discord: by making tints and shades (that is, by making colours lighter or darker), we can make colours which deviate from their natural chroma. Thus when we produce pink from red and orangey-brown from orange we can create a combination of orangey-brown and pink which is more interesting than simply putting orange and red together. This is to upset the natural tonal order of colours:

red, which is naturally the darker of the two, becomes pale, and orange, which is naturally the paler of the two, becomes dark. These are called 'discords' and do much to liven up what might otherwise be a fairly ordinary colour-scheme.

The colour-wheel

The colour-wheel (13) is simply a way of showing how the three primary colours combine with each other to make a wide range of other colours. Many different colours are possible, depending on the contributions in its make-up, and shades and tints can be produced from all of these.

To understand more fully the complementary and analogous colour schemes, try the following exercise (see 15): measure the diameter of the colour-wheel shown here and cut four circles of the same size from stiff paper. Divide these into eighteen segments. Now cut segments from these and label them as shown:

a to show only one segment;
b to show two pairs of segments opposite each other on the wheel;
c to show six segments all next to each other;
d to show three separate segments at equal distances apart.

Push a large pin through the centre of each circle and rest the point on the colour-wheel underneath. Now revolve the paper circles to find examples of the various types of colour schemes.

Whilst it is useful and interesting to know a certain amount about the theory of colour, do not feel that you must be ruled by it, nor should you let it intimidate you, only guide. There are many theories put forward by eminent artists, scientists, mathematicians and philosophers, all of them different. Even today, people who use colour for different purposes (painters, florists, graphic artists, embroiderers) use different words to express the same thing, and this may be confusing until you realize that there are no really hard and fast rules. Learning some colour theory does, however, open up new areas of discovery, especially for those who enjoy experimenting.

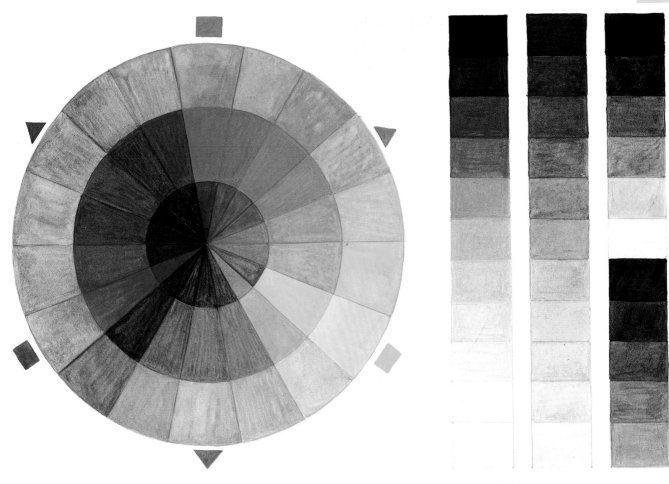

13 *The colour-wheel.*

14 *Neutral colour tones.*

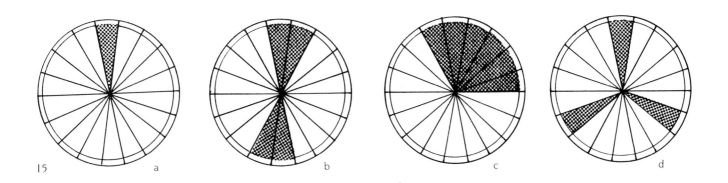

15   a   b   c   d

Experiment 1

Select threads in six colours which range through as many tones as possible. The six colours should include the three primaries and three secondaries. Cut six strips of card and stick double-sided adhesive tape on the back of each. Wrap the strips with your chosen threads to produce six coloured strips in graded tones.

Use these six strips as the basis of experiments to show analogous and complementary colour schemes. (You may need another set of coloured strips.) In 16 the original strips have been set alongside others having a *mixture* of those same colours, though here and there, tiny specks of the complementaries show through, making the schemes more interesting. This can also be done with the three lower examples by finding mixed threads which have something of both colours in them, and placing them alongside.

Begin to notice examples of analogous and complementary colour schemes: people's clothes, interior decorations, wrapping paper and cards, pictures and fabrics. Look back at the embroideries you have done in the past to see whether you have been playing safe with analogous colour schemes where you might have been more adventurous. Notice nature's colour schemes, too, which are not always 'safe' and easy on the eye. Using paints, threads, fabrics or coloured pencils, make notes of colour schemes and ideas from nature, and also collect cuttings from magazines which give you ideas for interesting colour schemes which you might not have thought of, even those which you do not like. In your notebook make headings such as *warm*, *cool*, *tints* (known generally as 'pastels'), *shades*, *happy* and *sad*, and collect and collate cuttings, photographs and materials under these headings to give you ideas for the future. Keep all material gathered in this way neatly arranged for easy reference.

16a

16b 'Colour Triangles' (detail), by Victoria Macleod. 69 × 72.5 × 72.5 cm (27 × 28½ × 28½ in.). A fascinating academic exercise in mixing the three primary colours by means of the surface embroidery on each of the small triangles. Some of these are decorated by hand and some by machine, while sequins, sequin waste, beads and ribbons add texture and pattern to the otherwise plain fabrics. Each piece is backed over card and the undersides covered with paler matching fabrics, and these have a line of buttonhole stitch along each horizontal edge to facilitate the linking stitches at each corner. This arrangement has infinite possibilities and is an excellent way of 'playing' with coloured shapes to alter their relationship to each other. (Photo: Jan Messent)

Experiment 2

(See 17) Base this experiment on a page from your scrapbook or from a photograph, leaf, flower, or other 'undesigned' source.

1 Choose a colour scheme (on a photograph or object) which appeals to you but which you have never used before, and try to identify all the colours and tones of colours in it. Look carefully at shadows, highlights, and tiny areas of pattern and detail.

2 Select threads and fabrics from your supply which correspond as nearly as possible with these colours. Using long narrow strips of card, as in the previous exercise, wind your chosen threads along the card *in the same proportions* as those in your picture. Snippets of fabric can be laid alongside, as shown.

3 Wrap another piece of card using the same threads (and fabrics too, if you wish), but this time, change the proportions to produce an entirely different effect. This exercise will help you to look for, and identify, colours

17

and to match them to threads and fabrics, to compare their tonal values and to estimate the various proportions and colour balances. It also helps to illustrate how schemes take on a different 'mood' when these proportions are changed, affecting their inter-relationship with each other.

Experiment 3

Take three different coloured background fabrics and mark a 10 cm (4 in.) square on each one. Select the six colours as in Experiment 1 and use any embroidery stitch which inter-locks (such as buttonhole, cretan, vandyke, herringbone), to work rows, either straight or curved, so that the colours overlap each other. Do this in any order, to find out what happens when two colours merge, and what effect the background colours have on the intensity of the coloured threads. You may notice in the two examples shown here (18) that the spaces between the stitches are more noticeable in the light version, thus highlighting the vertical lines of the arrangement, while in the dark version the horizontal wavy lines are more prominent.

Experiment 4

Now try a similar interlocking stitch version, but this time using several tones of only one colour. Take two pieces of background fabric in different colours (except black and white), the same size as before, and use an interlocking stitch in the same way as in Experiment 3 on both pieces of fabric, to discover what effect the background colour has on the colour of the threads. Some suggestions are:

- green threads on violet and red;
- green threads on yellow and blue;
- blue threads on orange and grey;
- red threads on blue and yellow-green;
- grey threads on red and blue-green.

You may find that the thread colours absorb a little of whatever background colour you put them on, and so look entirely different, even though they are actually the same.

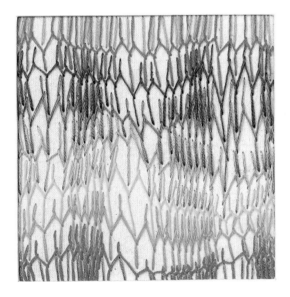

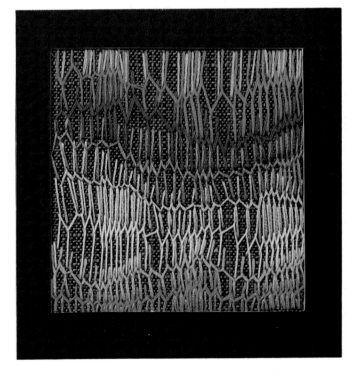

18

Project: colours of the seasons

The colours which we associate with the seasons of the year will depend on many factors, some of which will be determined by where we live, our age and personal memories, our state of mind, and so on. To some, spring means renewal, rebirth and joy, while others may think of it with pain. Whatever it means to you, choose one of the seasons and begin to collect helpful resource material such as photographs, flowers, leaves and garden catalogues, as well as coloured and patterned fabrics and threads.

Your experiment will be about 10 cm (4 in.) square, so decide which technique to use and collect the fabrics you will need for this. Canvas embroidery (or needlepoint) is useful for colour exercises; also cross stitch, appliqué and simple layering of fabrics with some stitchery.

1 Mark a 10 cm (4 in.) square on your chosen fabric using tacking stitches, and be prepared to combine techniques if you think this will produce a more interesting and lively effect.
2 Cut a strip of stiff card measuring 12.5 × 1.5 cm (5 in. × ½ in.) and place double-sided adhesive tape down one side. Using small samples of your chosen threads and fabrics, wrap the strip of card and place this either vertically or horizontally within your square as part of your design. (See 19 and 20.) Pin the strip in position and work a very simple design or pattern in your chosen technique and colours to represent one of the seasons.
3 The strip of wrapped card is stuck in position when the embroidery is complete. To mount each piece, choose a coloured heavy card which complements the colours in your embroidery, cut a square window in this of the same size, and place it over your embroidery. Check that it fits correctly, then glue carefully round the inside edge of the *card* and place it on top of the fabric and press down (20). Each sample you work may be regarded as an end in itself, or as the preliminary exercise to some larger work.

The use of wrapped strips, in this exercise, has its serious side and should not be regarded as a gimmick.

- For beginners, it helps to organize the colours at the outset of the exercise instead of leaving this to chance.
- It takes the embroiderer well in to the design stage without actually doing very much, and some may find this helpful. The fact that there are already some colours in position can be a great help in deciding quickly what part they should play in the design.
- It improves the worker's ability to regard the exercise as one which concerns *colour* and lessens the chances of habitually producing a *picture*. In other words, it introduces an abstract element, which is a help to many people.

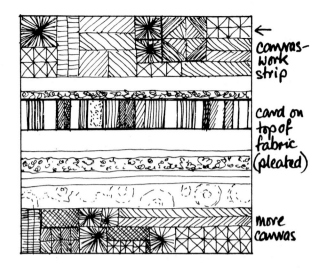

canvas-work strip ←

card on top of fabric (pleated)

more canvas

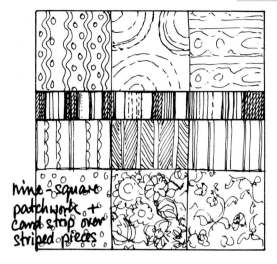

nine-square patchwork + card strip over striped pieces

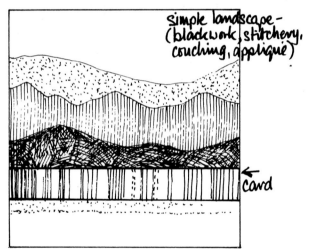

simple landscape- (blackwork, stitchery, couching, appliqué)

card ←

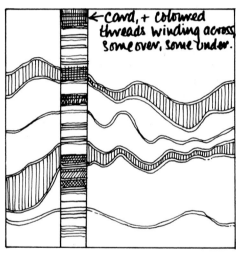

← card, + coloured threads winding across, some over, some under.

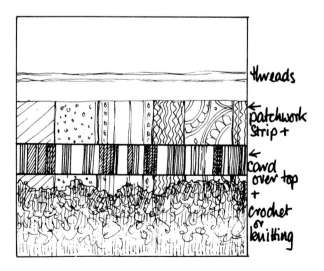

threads ←

patchwork strip + ←

card over top + crochet or knitting ←

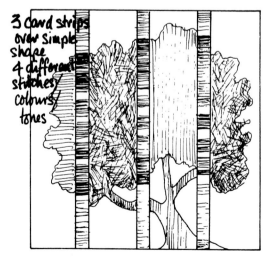

3 card strips over simple shape 4 different stitches, colours, tones

19

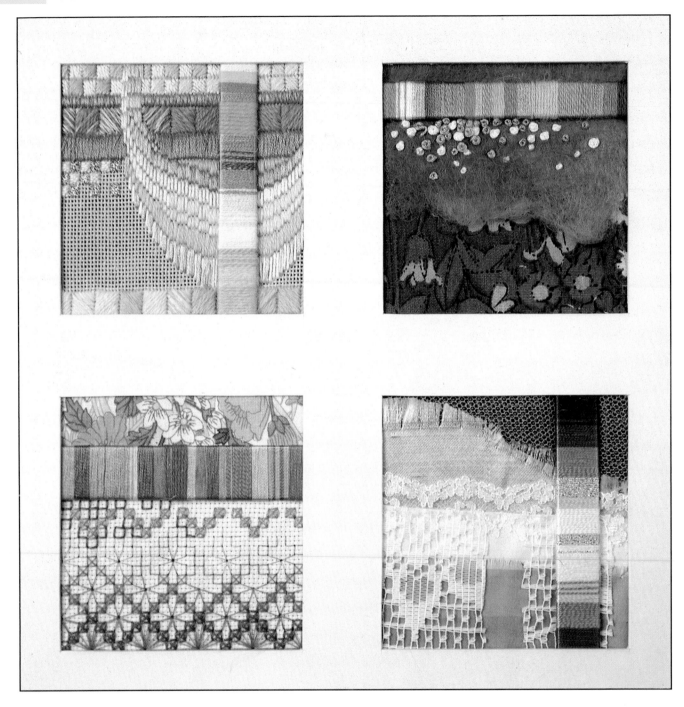

Colour symbolism

Our personal feelings about colour may well have been absorbed when we were very young, as a result, perhaps, of our attitudes towards people, places, things (liked and disliked) and deeply rooted emotions now forgotten. The symbolism attached to colours may, on the other hand, be the legacy of ancient beliefs passed down through the centuries, but it may actually help some of us to crystallize our thoughts about colours and to use them in new ways. It may, indeed, be what we need to give meaning and direction to future projects.

Project

Using books (perhaps in your local library), explore the symbolism of colour and plan a series of small embroideries to illustrate your findings. You may find this easier to achieve in an abstract form than through pictures, taking one stitch and one technique in tones of one colour to symbolize the meaning you wish to convey. You will discover that colours have many 'meanings', some of them quite contradictory, depending on the country of origin and their psychological and physiological connotations. Don't be put off by this; simply choose the interpretation *you* prefer and which you find easiest to suggest in an abstract design.

As work progresses on these small experimental pieces, it is almost certain that many other ideas will spring to mind for future development. Make a note of these ideas as they occur, like the sketches seen in 21 *a*, *b* and *c*, and stay with the subject until these ideas have been tried out in more detail. The ideas shown in these three sketches can be worked in a variety of techniques, either in a colour-scheme which symbolizes something to you, or in the colours of the seasons.

21

Painting on fabric

The use of paint can be of great help in providing colour in places where one does not wish (for a variety of reasons) to have the added texture of applied fabric or stitchery. In learning how best to use it, experiments are essential, as the combination of fabric, water, paint and threads may be, for you, a new experience for which a little practice may be needed. The main difference is the way in which the surface of the fabric accepts the paint: it may at first lie in little globules on top, it may spread far and wide along the fibres beyond the boundaries of your design, or it may pass straight through without a trace on to the surface below. This will depend upon the type of fabric you use, and the effects are part of the fun of experimenting.

There are various types of fabric colourants available, made by firms like Dylon, Reeves, and Winsor and Newton, and easily obtainable in the form of soft paints, crayons and paint sticks. They are easy and pleasant to use, and give good strong colours of any strength, though if you have some good artists' watercolours available you may wish to practise with these first on a small scale. Refer to the section on colour for help in mixing, and try out some of the following experiments.

- Use a selection of white or cream fabrics cut into smallish pieces: for example, sheeting, calico, lawn, muslin, organdie.
- Apply paint to *both* dry and wet fabrics to see what happens.
- Use different strengths of paint, some watery, some dry and thick.
- Use as many different tools as you can as well as the usual brushes, fine, rounded, flat, stiff and soft, on all the surfaces you have prepared.
- Try dropping paint on to the fabric, blowing it through a straw, and, if you have one, a spray. Do this on wet *and* dry surfaces.
- Use shaped pieces of card (templates) and windows (stencils) to mask off parts of the fabric while you apply colours to the outside, or inside, areas of the shape.
- Mix white with some colours and note how it gives more 'body'. It may produce a matt surface on a shiny fabric such as satin or silk.
- Notice how the wet colours are always darker until the fabric dries. Allow for this before deciding whether the result is acceptable or not.

Exercises in painting on fabric

1 23a shows white cotton with openwork stripes woven in. Very pale paint is used in the six divisions between these stripes, first on the tree areas, then on the

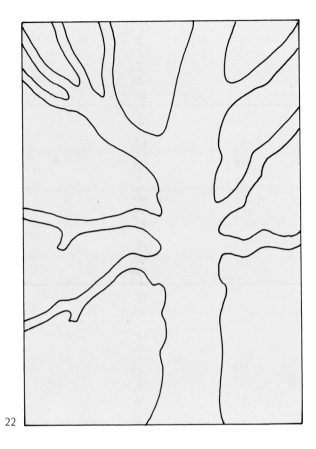

22

background areas, alternately. Tree outlined in split stitch with white stranded cotton, but this is not continued through woven stripes.

2 23b shows calico background painted in all areas around the tree in green (the negative spaces), then overlaid with blue/green organza and backstitched around the tree shape. Pockets thus formed stuffed with knitting yarn (a tubular nylon made by Phildar) in three different tones. Light wash of white paint applied to tree to accentuate the shape, though this also had the effect of creating a matt surface which contrasts well with the negative parts.

3 23c shows calico background with tree painted in pale green, deepening in tone towards the base. A narrow strip of white net gathered and sewn down the main trunk, and tiny snippets of gold/green lurex stitched at intervals underneath the edges. Fine gold thread satin-stitched irregularly across the boughs, and beads added. An offcut of blue patterned fabric at the base helps to add extra colour and balance.

4 23d shows calico background completely painted, the tree a deep, dull green and the background pale. Fence

a   b   c

d   e

23 *Exercises in paint and fabric.*

couched in shiny brown thread caught down at inter-sections. Leaves roughly worked in satin stitch and trunk given extra emphasis with layers of herringbone shading.

5 23e shows calico background completely covered in soft greens, leaving tree shape empty. Tree shape then accentuated in white and pale green threads in knotted and cable chain, coral and chain stitches. Background sprinkled with seeding for added textural interest.

24 'Winter Face'. 20.5 cm (8 in.) square. A plastic doll's face was used as the basis for this fantasy. The plastic base was covered with a rubber-based glue, then two layers of fine cotton fabric were stuck down into all the corners, completely covering the colours beneath. When this was dry, the face was then re-painted and the whole piece applied to a white background and embroidered with tiny pieces of applied fabrics, beads, sequins and stitching. (Courtesy of Sylvia Cosh)

3
Drawing and design development

Most people who have learned to do something will try to convince you that it was easy; this is our way of assuring each other that we are not really very clever, just determined. On the other hand there are many people who believe that *some* things cannot be learnt, that some can do it from the word 'go', whereas some never will. These are nearly always the people who can't! Both kinds are mistaken.

Drawing, painting and designing is not so very easy, not even for those who do it well. Behind each successful piece there are dozens which did not work, a lot of groans and despair. People who are good at drawing probably took many years to learn how to do it, and even then they have to keep practising, just like musicians or athletes. *It doesn't have to be easy to be enjoyable.*

If you ever learnt to read, write, play a musical instrument or drive a car, you can also learn to draw and design. You may not be an expert, but you *can* become proficient and you could even begin to enjoy it. Those people who practise their drawing regularly will always have the advantage over those who don't. Even if you do not actually use your drawings as part of your designing, it will teach you to observe and record, and these are disciplines which every designer needs, no matter how she actually produces her designs.

There is never only one way to develop a design; everyone has a different way of seeing things, so it is *critically important* that you do not regard the following examples as the only way of proceeding. These are the result of my thinking at this time; tomorrow I might do them differently. They merely represent possible lines of investigation.

Exercises in drawing

You may be one of those people who does the barest minimum of preparation for an embroidery, but there are still very good reasons why you should take time to draw regularly. Leaving aside those who draw for the sheer enjoyment of it, compare the discipline of drawing to the musician who must practise exercises to keep his fingers supple and to understand the structure of music at the same time. In the same way, drawing is not only a means of self-expression but also a way of learning how to look perceptively at things around us, and to take note of details, finding out how to record these discoveries, and in some strange way, discovering more about oneself. The fear that 'non-drawers' have is usually that whatever they draw will not look anything like their subject. They rarely try to explain this by saying that they haven't practised for twenty years, preferring to believe for some strange reason that their difficulties come about because they're not very clever. Now, this is patently nonsense, since they would not apply the same reasoning if asked to type an essay when they hadn't used a typewriter for twenty years! Anyone who practises drawing will get better at it, and most will become extremely proficient. Some will even discover that they enjoy it, and *everyone* will discover more about her own powers of perception and ability to record. Gradually, with daily practice, we begin to realize that ideas for design are forming from the things we look at more carefully, and that old excuse, 'I'm waiting for inspiration', will be seen for the nonsense that it is.

Designers don't need, or wait for, inspiration; they make it inside themselves. They don't need wonderful locations, or to live in the country, or more time, peace, money, etc. They sit down and draw things like these seen in 25, and *work* at designs. It doesn't flow out of their fingertips, it often has to be dragged out unwillingly, and worked at under the 'wrong' conditions until something materializes. It isn't always comfortable or easy. Remember, when you see a lovely design, that there were plenty of trials which were rejected and which you will never see. People only put their *best* ones on display.

Practice drawing small familiar things first, rather than landscapes and portraits.

- Acquire a collection of pencils, HB, B and BB, and try them out to see what kind of marks they make. Always keep them *very sharp*, using a craft knife.
- Use good cartridge paper to draw on: a sketch book is a good source of reference so find a useful size, not too small (unless you intend to keep it in a pocket or handbag), and don't rely on using a rubber: try to do without one.
- Draw with pens too, also fibre-tips, pastels, crayons and paint, and accustom yourself to making marks with them. Coloured pencils, especially the water-soluble kind, are very useful, particularly when it is not convenient to use ordinary paint.
- To increase your powers of observation and ability to record, stop 'doodling' from memory and tackle actual objects, such as:
an electric plug on the end of a wire
a telephone
a shoe or slipper
your other hand, or your foot (bare!)
a loosely arranged scarf, shawl or other drapery
someone's eye, ear, nose and mouth, separately, and from life
a lettuce or cabbage leaf
a piece of crumpled paper
a coil of string, wool or rope
a feather (however tattered)
a flower or plant which has reasonably large and simple leaf shapes
- Whenever possible, look at the drawings of artists such as Leonardo da Vinci, Holbein, Ingres, Charles Rennie Mackintosh and Eric Fraser. Notice their techniques, how they produce shading, their media and styles. Note how their techniques change according to the subject; in some cases their styles change too.

25

From design to embroidery

A design is not necessarily a picture

You can take a picture to pieces and reassemble it to make a design, but first you must examine it carefully to find out which are the 'best bits'.

Preliminary study is essential

Be as informed about the subject as you possibly can. This means collecting reference material from all sources and collating it.

Drawing aids the senses

You cannot rely entirely on your eyes and/or memory to provide all the facts you need about the design potential of your subject. You need to explore them now through paint, pencil, collage, etc, which will tell you more about lines, shapes, patterns, and so on.

You will not need to think of embroidery techniques yet

The examination of your subject need not be thought of as embroidery at this stage. You may now have to ask yourself these questions:

What are the strongest elements (i.e. the 'best bits') of the original idea which I like, and/or which have developed from my subsequent studies, drawings, paintings, etc.?

Are they the colours, the shapes, the patterns, the textures, anything else? Or are they combinations of some of these?

Experiment to explore the potential of these elements

You may not be able to put all the 'best bits' into the same design. This would be rather like adding all your favourite foods to the same dish! Now is the time to discover some ways of using the material you have acquired in different ways to see what works best, concentrating on your choice of elements (as above).

Recipe time: still no embroidery

You may find it difficult not to dash straight into the embroidery at this point, but *hold on*! If you want to make the most of the material you have prepared, now is the time to 'doodle' with your ideas, fit them into shapes, introduce those elements you find important, emphasize interesting parts, play down (or exclude) the bits you don't like. Make

these 'recipes' quite small. Watch the spaces, the shapes, the colours and textures, and balance all these together. Remember that you are designing, not necessarily making a picture.

At last – embroidery (but still only playing)

Now try out some of your 'recipes' in fabric and/or thread to see which materials and techniques will work, and, equally important, which will not. Make a few experiments to try out:

- several designs;
- several techniques;
- several different materials.

This is an important stage not to be excluded, as plans and designs on paper look different from the real thing and one needs experience to know whether they will work or not.

The real thing

Now you're totally confused. Too many good ideas. Help! If you have done all your preliminaries properly, you *will* have a great many more ideas than you can use: this is as it should be, and means that you can: (i) keep on using this subject for a long time until you feel that you have exhausted it, or (ii) keep it filed away until you need it for another project. In either case, the time you spent was not wasted. Just remember: *don't put all your good ideas into one piece!* Take one good idea which fits all your requirements, or combine one or two ideas from the various experiments, and carry them out in the way your experiments led you to believe would work. Keep it simple and stick to the subject; give it a chance to work out.

Help! It's not working

You are about one-quarter to one-third of the way into your embroidery. It looks nothing like you hoped or expected it to be at this stage. What went wrong? *Nothing.* Have faith and develop vision. Few things in their elementary and unformed stages look anything like the finished articles, simply because they *are* unformed and unfinished. Keep going in exactly the way you planned (those who missed out the preparatory stages can expect more hiccoughs than the rest of us!). Of course, there will be lots of details to add and changes made here and there. We are 'creating' all the way through, but don't be panicked into thinking that it was all a terrible mistake: keep going and give it a chance. If you were quite pleased with your plan, you must have the confidence to carry it through.

T pen-sketch of poppy heads
coloured pencil (water soluble)
sketch of poppies minus leaves —

leaf
crinkles

26

a

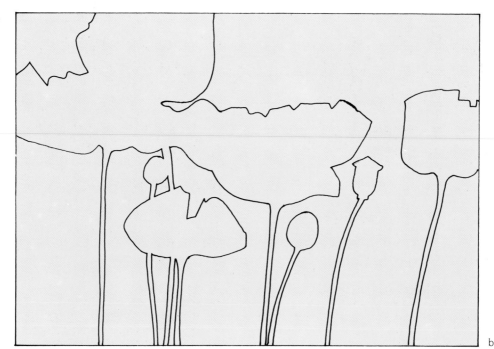

27

b

c

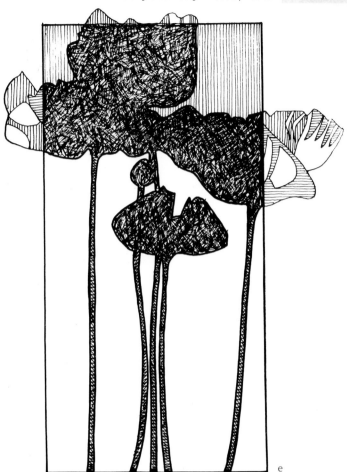

e

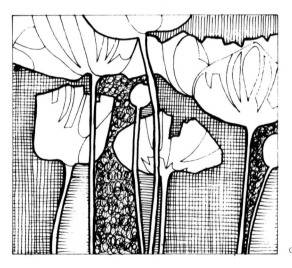

d

Design developments from the poppies in *26*

As I work from the sketches of the poppies, I try various arrangements to see how ideas can be produced and 'recipes' made from these ideas. The sketches shown here do not necessarily follow in a logical progression one from the other, but show how certain lines developed to produce a selection of possible designs. In the end, I may choose none of them, and may try to incorporate the best

bits of one or two, but until I have tried to sift through some ideas (27), I shall not know how best to begin.

a The shapes made most impact, even more than colour, so I traced the shapes from the drawing, including the little orange shapes inside the petals, as these looked very interesting.

b The shapes are enclosed inside a rectangle which cuts off some of the petals and thus produces a series of interesting background shapes.

c Now a different-sized rectangle with the previous details too, but this left no room for the flowers at the right, so these were moved into the space on the left. Extra seed head excluded.

d Another rectangle, focusing attention on the background shapes.

e Now concentrating solely on flat shapes of flowers against the white shapes of the background inside an elongated rectangle. Decided to allow the flowers to 'fall out' at lower left.

41

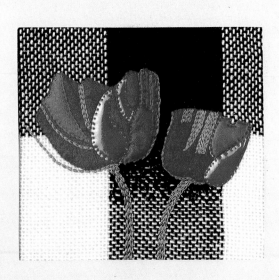

28a *Appliqué on a check fabric. 2.36 cm (6 in.) square.*

28b *Shadow quilting. 2.36 cm (6 in.) square.*

The trial embroidery stage

After the drawing and designing stages comes the experimental work to discover how one may translate the ideas into fabric and thread. Only two of the poppy heads were used in my experiments, as I needed to find out whether the techniques I had in mind would actually work with this type of design, and whether it needed to be made larger. My main interest was in the shapes of the flowers, the colour being of secondary importance, but I decided for the moment to keep to reds for the sake of recognition.

My discoveries

The two poppy heads were scaled up (i.e. made larger), but even so, the small pieces needed for appliqué and shadow quilting were very fiddly. Some even had to be omitted altogether for this reason, though if the design had been on a much larger scale, this would not have been a problem. Applied fabrics were all non-fraying: felt, leather and shiny PVC.

I liked the effect of the black and white check fabric in the appliqué experiment, and by using french knots the black square was made to overflow downwards, which accentuated the shapes of the poppy heads. Altogether an exciting combination of shapes and colours, but I felt that

I would like to introduce more pattern somewhere, perhaps different-sized checks.

The shadow quilting shows coloured felt pieces sandwiched between shot blue/red organdie and white cotton. This alone produced a rather bland effect, so I experimented by laying a selection of transparent fabrics over part of the embroidery to add more tones and textures, and found that two layers of mauve/pink lurex fabric made a big difference. The transparent quality allows the design to disappear towards the bottom. The pieces were re-quilted over the second fabric.

Many more ideas came to mind as work proceeded, though I realized that the scale would dictate which ones would work best with which technique. An all-white design appealed to me, and one using layer upon layer of transparent fabrics, but canvas work (or needlepoint) was a technique I particularly wanted to try. Taking the pattern element from the black, white and red design, and the colour element from the shadow quilting design, I worked a canvas embroidery on very fine canvas (18s), with the addition of applied pieces to create areas of flat texture. For this, pieces of fabric-covered card and soft leather were used, stitched on to the canvas after the stitchery was in place (29).

29 Canvas and fabric. 2.36 cm (6 in.) square.

Project 1

In the photograph opposite (30*b*) you see an arrangement of rectangles of different sizes and shapes, interlocking and creating a pattern of greys, black, creams and browns. This is, in fact, part of the back wall of a cottage which, because of its age, combines a variety of building materials with a not-too-strict accuracy. If you can see this picture simply as a pattern rather than a building, you will understand its potential as an embroidery design.

Make two large L shapes from stiff paper (white is best) and cut them out (30*a*). Use these as moveable frames to enclose the picture, cutting off any part of it which you prefer not to use – the right-hand edge, perhaps? When you have found a suitable arrangement, draw the size and shape of this on another piece of paper and use it for a new drawing of the design inside your frame, simplifying those shapes which need to be made clearer, and noting all the various lines and shapes as they occur. You may wish to straighten, lengthen or shorten some of them to balance your design. This is allowed! If you still want your design to look like a building, you could show a cat curled up on the windowsill, or a vase of flowers, or an oil-lamp.

At this stage you may wish to continue experimenting with the design, to try various arrangements and sizes, and to make decisions about techniques. Suggestions for this type of design: canvas work, blackwork and pulled thread, appliqué, quilting and cutwork or any combination of these, perhaps with the use of paint too.

30*b* (Photo: Jan Messent)

```
←——————— ABOUT   20 CMS. ———————→

CUT TWO PIECES THE SAME SIZE AND USE THEM TO MAKE "WINDOWS"
```

30*a*

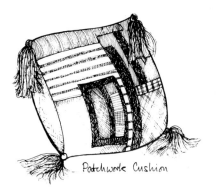

Patchwork Cushion

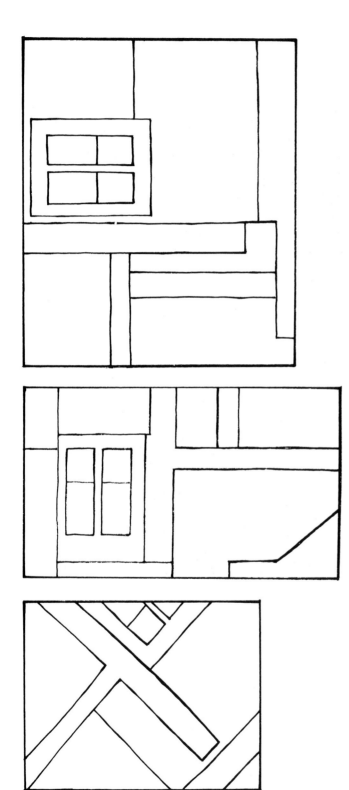

Project 2

The sinuous curves and twisting lines seen on agate (31) are quite different from the straight rectangular pattern of walls, and provide ideas for an embroidery of quite another kind. Use the L-shaped frames again for this design, to capture a small part of the photograph. You may wish to draw small parts of the agate just for practice, and then translate some of your drawings immediately into stitchery, layers of fabric or corded quilting. After making some preliminary drawings, you may decide that the design will have to be either (i) enlarged, and/or (ii) simplified, so decide which lines or shapes can be eliminated without spoiling the beauty of the arrangement.

As a continuation of both of these projects, make sketches and finished drawings to show how some of your designs could be put to some practical use, either on dress, accessories, cushions or other household items such as a bed-head cover, or a jewellery box.

31 A *polished slice of agate.* (Photo: Jan Messent)

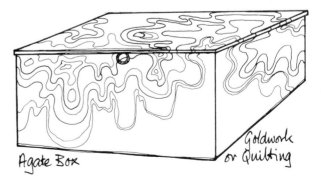

Agate Box

Goldwork or Quilting

45

32 'Texture Tubes', by Victoria Macleod. 38 × 55 cm (15 × 21½ in.). A highly textured and interesting embroidery worked entirely in one fabric, made by Victoria for her City and Guilds Part II examination in 1986. Among the plain and flatter padded pieces and Suffolk puffs are the bolder and larger examples of smocking, pleating, tucking and corded quilting. These are all shaped around 'pill-boxes' of foam and card.

4
Fabrics

Ideally, one should aim to have as wide a range as possible of fabrics with which to experiment, some fine, some soft, stiff, shiny, matt, smooth, textured and so on. It is always useful to sort them out into colours and keep them in separate bags; this will give you the experience, too, of handling them and deciding what else you need to balance the variety. Unbleached calico and good white sheeting are very useful for experiments; they are still quite cheap and are widely used by embroiderers for many techniques. They also accept paint very well. Felt is useful for occasions when fraying would be a nuisance, and fine transparent fabrics (even bits of net and lace) give interesting effects when laid over other materials. Keep tiny bits of braid, cord, lace and edgings in a separate bag: they can be used for pattern-making exercises. Keep bits of real silk and lurex for special effects, too, and don't discard rough pieces of hessian and window-cleaning scrim, as these have their uses. While you are sorting out your fabrics, you will discover gaps in the variety which should be filled. Is there too much thick, textured fabric and not enough plain cotton? Are there any transparent and delicate materials, or nets and small pieces of silk? Remember that you can ask for as little as ten centimetres of fabric when shopping for small pieces, and remnants trays often have very useful fabrics, plain and patterned, which cost much less than the usual price. Look for curtain fabric remnants too, as dupion and heavy cottons and satins make good backgrounds.

In this chapter, we shall be experimenting to *make* fabrics, *destroy* them, and *manipulate* them. This is all good practice to help us understand the behaviour of fabrics, and also provides a springboard from which other ideas can take off. If we tackle it in a disciplined way, it should help to show how ideas can begin from the fabric alone (that is, without any outside stimulus), and this may be the start of a long-term project. It need hardly be said that these are only basic ideas and that there are dozens more which could develop from them.

Fabric-making
A quick and easy way to make felt for experimental purposes

You will need about half a carrier bag full of clean fleece, ready-carded. If you want coloured felt, the fleece should be dyed beforehand, or alternatively you can sprinkle dyes on to it while it is still wet after the felting process. Experiment! You will also need two pieces of clean cotton fabric (calico or old sheeting) measuring about 30 cm (12 in.) square, a needle and some thread, boiling water, a washing-up bowl and an iron.

1 Pull the fleece into tufts, and lay some of them on top of one of the pieces of cotton, keeping well away from the edges and making an even layer. Do the same with all the fleece, layering it evenly in different directions until you have a neat flat pile.
2 Place the other cotton piece on top of this and hold it all down while you tack right through the complete pile with large stitches several times in each direction to hold the fleece firmly in place. Tack all round the edges too.
3 Place this parcel in the bowl and pour a kettle-full of boiling water over it while poking the parcel fiercely with a wooden spoon. If you have an old-fashioned potato-masher, this is the ideal tool generally to mistreat the wool while the fibres open up and tangle together. Agitate the wool parcel in the water by pressing and squeezing for about ten minutes.
4 Remove the parcel, plunge it into cold water, agitate again and then wring out by hand. Dry flat in the sun, or other warm place, or, if you're in a hurry, put it into the tumble-dryer until it is nearly dry.
5 Remove the tacking threads and peel off the cotton squares. Now replace them loosely on top of the felt and press firmly under a hot iron on both sides until quite flat and firm.

This will produce a smallish piece of felt to experiment with. Remember that part of the process involves shrinkage, so if you require larger pieces you should examine more orthodox methods of production. There are several good methods to try.

Discover as many ways as you can of making your own fabric, using either raw materials, 'waste' materials, yarns or recycled fabrics. Make a list of all the methods you know which produce fabrics, e.g. weaving, felting, knitting, knotting, netting, crochet, lace-making, plaiting, etc. Apply these methods to your own constructions as freely as possible, with the addition (if you wish) of sewing, sticking, and embroidery. Remember that the fabrics you produce need not be washable or hard-wearing.

The examples on the opposite page are made in the following ways:

1 (33*a*) Knotting made from strips of frayed and machined fabric with transparent plastic, the latter tied loosely together and flattened. (*Mary Holden*)
2 (33*b*) Needleweaving on a silk base using various threads and frayed strips of silk. The texture is varied by the use of heavier and finer areas of weaving.
3 (33*c*) Knitting with fine wool on fine needles in a simple pattern of vertical holes. These holes were then used as the 'ladders' for raised chain band in a random-dyed silk thread, and these were later pulled together in pairs to show the metallic fabric underneath.
4 (33*d*) Darning with narrow strips of fabrics and threads through two layers of curtain net, allowed to bulge out here and there to add to the surface texture.
5 (33*e*) Felting, made of pale green fleece containing tiny snippets of fabrics and lace motifs. The fine glitter thread is couched on top, and french knots added.
6 (33*f*) Crochet with fine yarn and hook to make a mesh of square holes (simple filet crochet), which are then used for *weaving* with textured yarns, silks, strips of fabric, plaits and cords. Crochet chains and french knitting can also be used as the weaving thread.
7 (33*g*) Plaiting narrow strips of fabric in tight braids which are then *woven* together to form a firm fabric.

Materials to experiment with: raw fleece, (dyed, natural or white); warp and weft threads removed from fabric; ribbons and lace edgings; cords, string and twine; plastic tubing; pipe cleaners; laces; leather thongs; strips of plastic carrier bags . . . disposable household cleaning cloths (cut up); net curtains; metal foil, especially the softer variety used for lining coffee packets; and tubular knitting yarns which have been 'filled' with something else such as another yarn, fabric or plastic waste.

Combine any of the illustrated examples, for example:

* Plait strips of handmade cords with handmade felt then weave these together.
* Crochet or knit with handmade cords, french knitting or crochet chains.
* Make felt and include pieces of textured yarns, shiny plastic bits, net and lace.
* Use macramé techniques and pure wool yarn to make a closely woven mesh, then try felting this to make it bond more firmly.
* Weave with a combination of knitting and macramé.

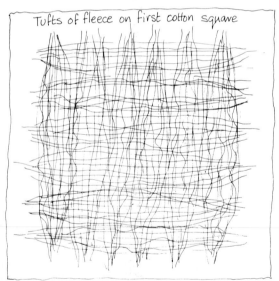

Tufts of fleece on first cotton square

Place second cotton square on top.

a

b

c

d

e

f

g

34 *Lakeside. (Photo: Jan Messent)*

Fabric destruction

Traditional embroidery techniques in which the warp and weft threads of woven fabric are pulled, withdrawn, cut and generally removed from their original position are numerous, and include some of the most satisfying and aesthetically pleasing methods to work. Alongside these traditional methods of reorganizing the threads are others which take things a little further into the realms of 'fabric destruction', and in which it is possible to produce exciting and unorthodox textural effects. This is an area where personal experimentation is vital, for there is no instruction book which will show you the step-by-step moves: it all depends on the effect you wish to create.

Go into these 'destruction' methods on the understanding that your time and fabrics are not being wasted if the results are less than satisfactory. This happens to the best embroiderers as well as to students, so be prepared to chop up and fray, to tear and rip, to snip and discard without worrying that 'it doesn't look like anything'. It won't: it is an experiment in learning what fabrics will and will not do, and this is valuable experience. Keep the results in your notebook.

- It may help you to have a photograph showing clear textural interest, like the one at the top of the opposite page, on which you might base an experiment. Let the textures suggest the method. Make a list of words in your notebook, such as *pull*, *cut*, *snip*, *tear*, *slash*, *fray*, *withdraw*. There are others too, which you might try (with caution!), such as *burn* and *dissolve*.
- Sort some of your fabrics into groups: those which will fray well, loosely woven fabrics, felts, and so on. These will almost certainly give you ideas as you handle them.
- Have some calico or sheeting handy for backing experiments if needed, also an embroidery hoop or simple frame, scissors and tough threads for tying.

35

The photograph above (35) is a rough fabric sketch based on the waterside scene opposite. Rough hessians and loosely woven scrim were frayed to simulate the dry reeds, then laid over shiny lining fabric and some chopped net. Your experiments may be totally abstract – this is perfectly valid – or, if you prefer, your work may be based on the ideas seen on the pattern pages ahead.

36 'Pink Bed Box', by Victoria Macleod. 27 × 20 cm (10½ × 8 in.). Any box-shaped piece of furniture will lend itself to this idea, and this one was made for a relation who was an employee of a well-known bed firm. The quilt and pillows lift off in one piece to form the lid, showing the inside which is padded in pink satin. Handmade needlepoint lace decorates the edges of the tiny pillows and the hexagonal patchwork quilt is made of delicately printed cottons. Round the top edge of the mattress, a handmade braid of cross stitch hearts trims the pink flounce, and the quilted velvet headboard is stiffened by a sandwich of stiff card.

37 (*Photo: Jan Messent*)

38 (*Photo: Jan Messent*)

Fabric manipulation

Manipulate fabrics to change the surface texture. Tree-bark is a well-worn source of inspiration for embroiderers, and yet still seems to provide a never-ending supply of material. Figs 37 and 38 instantly suggest fabric, perhaps chopped up and reassembled, cut organdie and net peeling away from rolled-up velvet . . . .

Try some small experiments based on these ideas and make a note also of these more unconventional fabrics and materials which might be used:

- medical gauze and bandages; good for different densities, for pulling about and 'scrunching';
- window-cleaning scrim: good for pulled thread and rough drawn thread work, for fraying and padding;
- net vegetable bags: as a foundation for threading other things through;
- machine knitting: stretchy and good for all kinds of manipulation;
- leathers, including chamois: stretches well, use both sides;
- foam pieces: very useful for padding;
- corn plasters, also good for padding, as are the polystyrene shapes used for packing.

Don't be tempted to use more than one good idea on an experimental piece, otherwise it may become fiddly and messy, and lose impact. Mount each exercise on matching card, with its inspirational source if possible, and put this into your notebook or portfolio. Make a collection of ideas from cuttings and photographs of textures which may suggest fabric manipulation possibilities, and keep these with your experiments and notes.

Experiments

Ideas for texture experiments are all around us. Those seen on the facing page include roof tiles, trailing stems and leaves in a greenhouse, the branches of a cedar tree seen from below, the fleshy leaves of a garden plant, tiny fat leaves of the sedum plant, the velvety ruffles of a bracket fungus, and water skimming the tops of flat, smooth stones in a river. Sketch or photograph ideas like this as a basis for fabric experiments using any of the methods suggested on the previous pages.

1 Roof tiles: squares of felt or soft leather, curved and stitched over lines of soft cord or thick string.
2 Trailing stems over shadowy leaves: corded quilting over shadow quilting.
3 The cedar tree branches: a mixture of cutwork and roughly pulled threads, or needleweaving.
4 Large garden plant leaves: individually cut leaf shapes of two fabrics (i.e. top and underside) with stiffening between, and quilted veins.
5 Tiny sedum leaves: background of ruched fabric, or gathered in two directions to pucker into little bumps. Make larger leaves separately.
6 Bracket fungus: velvet and felt closely resemble the texture of this plant, with closely stitched lines slightly puckering the surface.
7 Water over stones: make stones and pebbles of various smooth fabrics so that no wrinkles show. Use felt, velvet, satin, knitted fabric, with some handstitching for lines and textures where the colours change. Arrange the stones closely together and use transparent fabrics, stitchery and fine threads for the water. Water can also be made from shiny plastic materials, ribbons and metallic threads.

To conclude these ideas, make drawings to show how your experiments might be developed on a project to do with fashion or the home. Think of them as extending around necklines, cuffs and hems; down the fronts of evening jackets; on bags, belts or cushions; and on bed coverlets with a day-pillow cover to match.

39

Project 1: 'First catch your Brussels sprout . . .'

The brassica family have beautiful fleshy leaves and flowering bodies perfect for fabric embroidery (as opposed to stitchery and thread). Think of curly dark green cabbages, red and ornamental ones, kale and broccoli, cauliflowers with their decorative florets and the richly complicated folds of the tight white cabbage. The complete sprout plant opposite shows how, underneath the fleshy dark green leaves, the miniature cabbages are held tight and firm by the stem at the top, gradually becoming looser and larger towards the bottom. Make these wholly or partly three-dimensional from padded balls covered with separate leaves and fasten them on to a fabric-covered stem. Keep all stitches in scale with the size of the plant and pay great attention to subtle colour-changes.

If possible, have an actual plant in front of you to study and examine in detail. Do not rush into things before you have looked, made notes, sketched some parts, and have understood exactly how the plant is constructed. Try out some experimental pieces first to discover the best way of expressing the textures.

Gather fabrics which you feel have some relationship to the colours and textures of the plant: satins and velvets, and some chiffons and nets for minute colour-changes of blue to blue/green and white to cream. You may need Vilene for stiffening and a large selection of threads for extra textures and surface detail.

Draw how you will construct the base/foundation: you may have to make a small trial piece to see if your plans will actually work, using a variety of fabrics.

Look at the ideas on fabric manipulation and destruction to suggest possible translations. Collect other pictures of the brassica family, and take photographs of the plant you are using (if it is a fresh one) to remind you of the shapes and colours before it is consumed! Put all notes and sketches into your notebook so that it is all to hand when you need it, together with samples of the fabrics and threads used on the project. Photograph the various stages of construction, too, or sketch them, so that you are reminded of this for future projects, and also record the finished item. *Note:* if there is a danger that it may be mistaken for the real thing, keep it well away from the kitchen!

40

41 (Photo: V.A. Campbell-Harding)

Project 2

The tiled roof of a building in the Dordogne, photographed by Valerie Campbell-Harding (46), could be successfully reconstructed in fabric, perhaps as continuous horizontal strips, tucked, pleated and piped, or as layers of leather, felt, knitting or painted fabric. Try several experiments to discover ways in which this could be achieved without any preliminary drawing or design work. Keep all these experiments together with (if possible) a photostat of the photograph to remind you of the origin of the idea; this may then be incorporated into a different piece of work at some time in the future.

Project 3

A waterfall at Odda in Norway (42) provides an opportunity for a much freer use of fabrics and/or stitchery. The use of fine medical gauze is particularly useful in creating water effects, as it can very easily be pulled out and frayed to the required density. The rocks would translate well into overlaid and/or padded fabrics, and paint could be used here, too. Work several small experiments to create an impression of falling water; use any of the ideas mentioned above, and then create some of your own. Collect photographs and sketches of waterfalls to begin a file.

42 Waterfall at Odda, Norway. (Photo: John Hetherington)

5
Stitches

Perhaps more has been written about this aspect of embroidery than any other, and every student of embroidery should have at least one good manual of stitches to which she can refer for ideas and information.

For the purposes of discovery for its own sake, let us forget about the decoration of functional objects and concentrate, in this chapter, solely on experiments to find out more about stitches and our own powers of inventiveness. You may think that it will be difficult not to repeat what someone else has already done somewhere, but look at the following list of choices and ask yourself whether, with all the permutations possible, your concern is still justified.

Your choices are:

- colour;
- thread;
- stitch;
- density/scale;
- direction (movement or static?);
- pattern/texture;
- fabric (makes a difference to how stitches are used).

Any combination of these choices will produce a different effect, and each person will add her own interpretation according to the fabric on which she is working and the way she feels at the time. To discover more about stitches, first learn how they are grouped so that the choices you make are less random and more informed.

Exercise 1

Using a good stitch book, make lists of stitches which fall under these headings (put each group-list on a separate page of your notebook so that you can add to it and make notes).

1 Line stitches – these make single lines useful for outlining and drawing.

2 Building, or flat, stitches can be built up to cover large areas.
3 Knotted stitches are either in single units or lines, and are not smooth.
4 Looped stitches are made by looping the thread under the needle at some stage.
5 Chained stitches have many variations giving a decorative raised line but can also be used as filling stitches.
6 Filling stitches can be taken from all groups to fill in areas of varying densities.
7 Composite stitches are those made in more than one stage, sometimes in different threads.
8 Couching stitches are used to hold down threads which lie on the surface of the fabric. Stitches from the other groups can be used for this, as well as special ones.

Exercise 2

Now check through your materials. To be able to give scope to your experiments, you will need:

1 A good selection of threads*. Try to gather some of the following: stranded cotton, linen, cotton perlé, coton à broder, silks and rayons, crewel wool and knitting yarns (all thicknesses), machine threads, string, raffia, cords and narrow ribbons, torn strips of fabric and tape, etc.
2 All the necessary needles to take the above threads, from very fine to very large packing needles.
3 Fabrics. Don't just think in terms of special embroidery fabrics; use a wider variety of plain pieces, like soft cottons, curtain fabrics, hessian (burlap) and calico. If you have to buy extra pieces for your experiments, try to match the colours to your threads. Dress-weight woollens are also useful and easy to sew on.
4 You may need one or two embroidery hoops for these exercises, and a table-clamp will be useful too so that both hands are free to stitch.

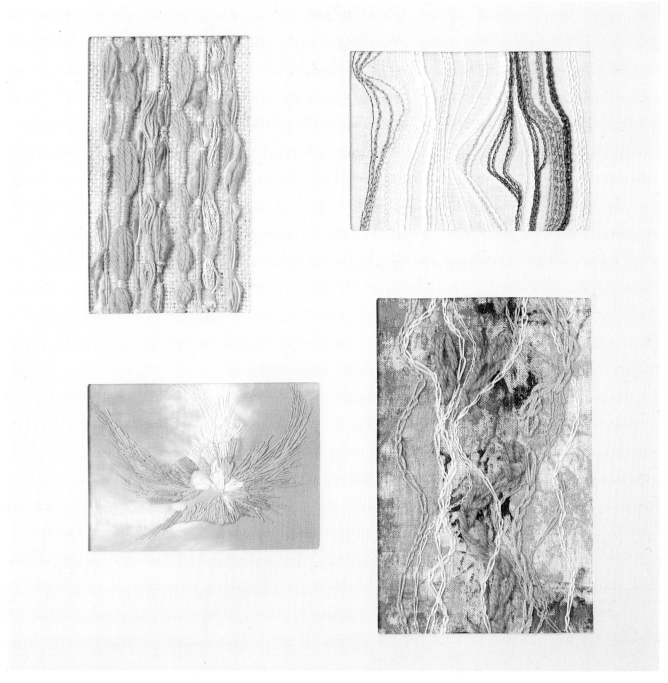

43

*(Note: if you are buying new threads in these varieties, concentrate on a limited number of colours, or keep to analogous or complementary colour schemes.)

Exercise 3

Select one stitch, preferably one with which you are not over-familiar, then choose a good selection of threads of all types in colours which will form a definite scheme when placed against the fabrics you wish to work on. (Use smallish pieces, about the size of this page.) Now try out your chosen stitch in a variety of different threads on several different fabrics. The examples opposite (43) show experiments worked in this way: on the right-hand side the stitches used are mainly chain stitch, stem and backstitch, and on the left, straight stitches are used for couching on hessian and as a way of indicating movement. The two lower pieces of fabric are tie-dyed and painted.

While you are working with your chosen stitch, refer to your list of choices (above) and make decisions which will help to achieve the effect you are seeking – delicacy or roughness, pattern or texture, large or small-scale and so on. You will find that the fabric you choose will play a greater part in the result than you had imagined. Keep these experiments as reference in your notebook, and do the same exercise with other stitches from other groups so that you eventually build up a library of ideas for future projects.

Project 1

This could be regarded as a development from the previous exercises, as it is a chance to put the ideas you have discovered to some use. Using one of the same stitches as before, embroider a small panel about 20-25 cm (8-10 in.) square of a simple landscape straight on to the fabric, omitting the drawing/designing stage. The example here (45) shows how this can be done by making undulating lines across to represent the foreground, middle distance, far distance and sky, allowing the background fabric to show through as part of the effect. Stitches are piled up on top of each other, layer upon layer, or thinned out to almost nothing.

Project 2

Again using the same stitch, work another panel of the same size (use either the same or a different colour scheme), but this time work entirely in pattern. Refer to the chapter on pattern, or draw some ideas on paper like those shown here (44) and then try to follow them in your chosen stitch. You may find that some patterns have to be adapted as you go along, or the scale changed, or you may need to introduce another stitch for interest – french knots, for example. It may also help to work on a patterned fabric such as a large check.

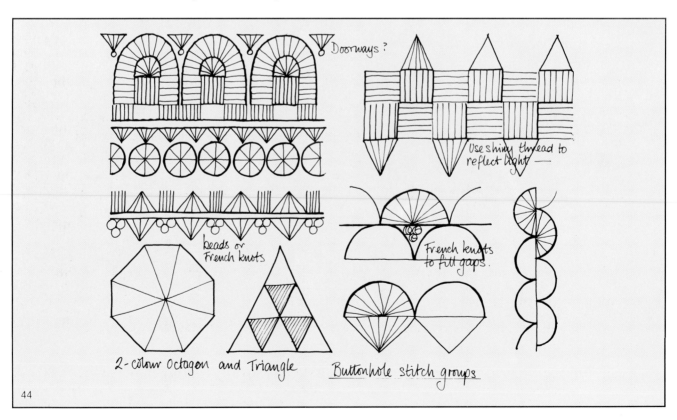

Doorways?

Use shiny thread to reflect light

beads or French knots

French knots to fill gaps.

2-colour Octagon and Triangle

Buttonhole stitch groups

44

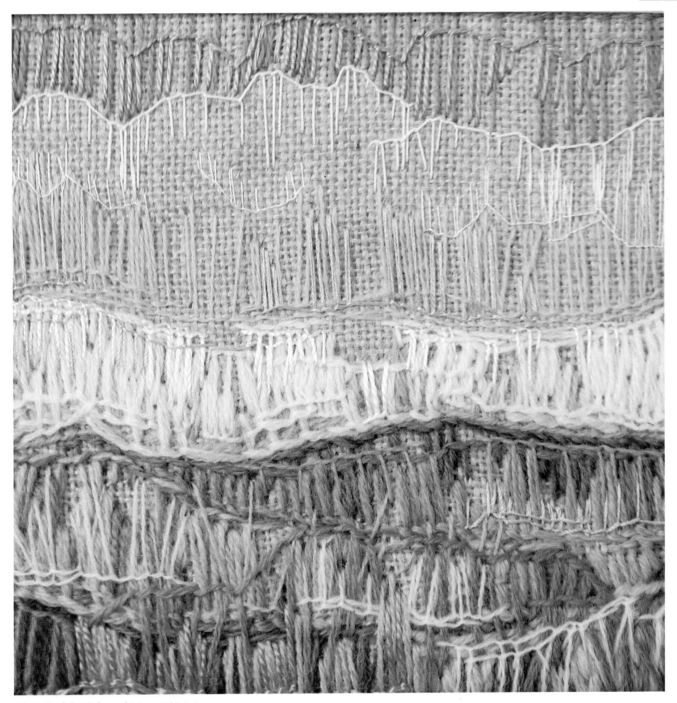

45 *Buttonhole stitch panel 14 cm (5 ½ in.) square.*

The object of the exercise is to learn how to exploit stitches more fully, and to find out more about their potential, in order to increase our inventiveness. If we always rely on chain, stem or back stitch to make a line, we shall never discover the countless line effects which can be made by other stitches. The combination of stitches and

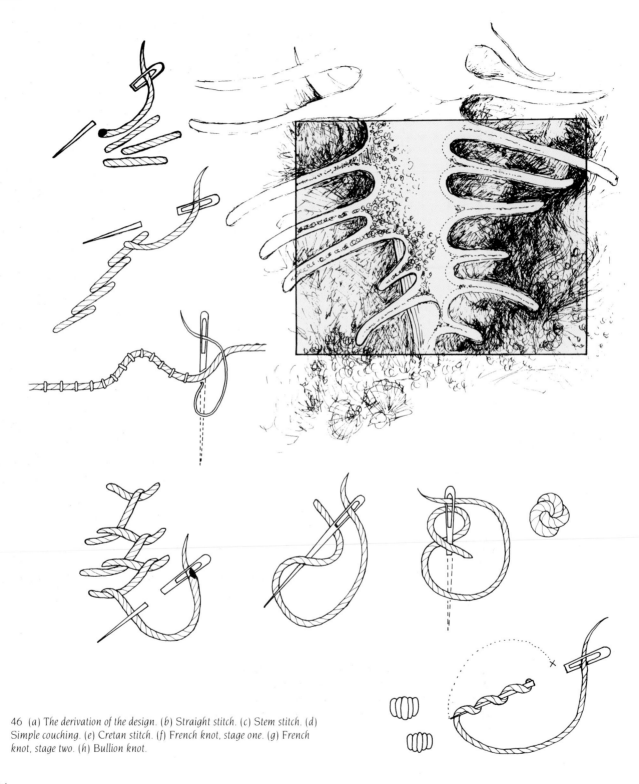

46 (a) The derivation of the design. (b) Straight stitch. (c) Stem stitch. (d) Simple couching. (e) Cretan stitch. (f) French knot, stage one. (g) French knot, stage two. (h) Bullion knot.

47 'Shell', by Mary Holden. 11.5 × 13 cm (4½ × 5 in.).

design need not be a complicated affair: if you did the previous landscape exercise without the usual planning stages, you will no doubt have enjoyed the fun of allowing the stitches themselves to dictate the texture and design. This exercise is a step further on.

The embroidery on this page (47) is by Mary Holden and shows a small portion of a spiny shell in a bed of seaweed.

To enclose the design area and isolate it from the rest of the picture, Mary used the two L-shaped pieces of paper (see page 44) to find a pleasing arrangement of shapes. The drawing on the opposite page shows the stitches she used: try to identify these in the embroidery. Size of embroidery: 12.5 × 11 cm (5 × 4½ in.).

Jean's bean patch. Bolkloy. '85.

48

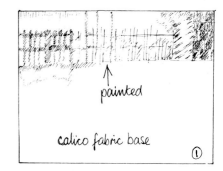

painted

calico fabric base

①

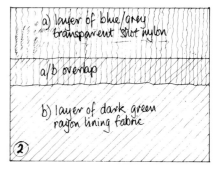

a) layer of blue/grey transparent slot nylon

a/b overlap

b) layer of dark green rayon lining fabric

②

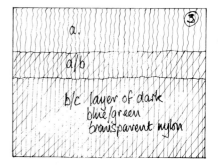

a.

a/b

b/c layer of dark blue/green transparent nylon

③

④

a.

a/b

a narrow strip of lurex net

b/c

Project 3

Choose a similar picture (a photograph or magazine cutting) showing an example of static lines against a background of movement and texture, such as:

- a simple figure shape against blurred traffic images or lines;
- sheep outlined against wind-blown trees;
- fish against moving water plants (or water alone).

Now use the L-shaped paper frames to enclose the most interesting part, but keep the design simple and well balanced. Transfer the outlines to tracing paper, adjust any parts which need to be changed and then transfer the design on to a suitable fabric, bearing in mind the stitches and threads you intend to use, and the colours. If possible, use the stitches with which you have already experimented.

'Jean's Bean Patch' (49) is an example of how paint, fabric and stitches can be used together to create colour and texture. The sketch, shown above, was made early in the morning in summer, when the sun was still quite low in the sky. The light was shimmering softly through the fence and on to the palest bean-leaves, creating a translucent effect

with the dried grass and distant lacy trees. Particularly appealing was the pattern of fence, garden chairs, tiles and stonework (at the right), moving across the top of the scene in contrast to the haphazard texture of the plants. Pen-and-

49 'Jean's Bean Patch'. 20.5 × 23 cm (8 × 9 in.). (Courtesy of Jean Dalglish.)

ink sketches and photographs are both useful for reference as aids to one's memory.

The diagrams opposite explain how the layers of fine transparent fabrics were overlaid on a base of unbleached calico which had been painted across the top using ordinary watercolour paints. The fabric softened the harder edges of the paint, giving the effect of soft diffused light at the top and, at the bottom, depth of colour. Some stitchery (straight stitch and seeding) was worked over the paint to accentuate details; all other stitches are straight, using stranded cottons, perlé and fine machine threads.

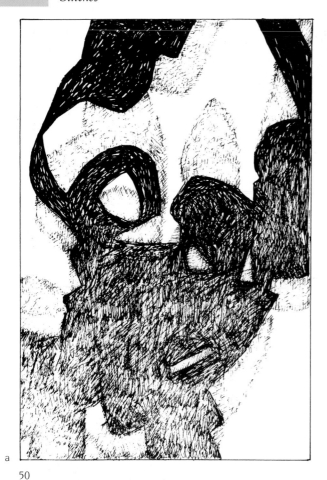

a

50

b

c

Project 4

Refer again to the seven choices at the beginning of the chapter and then apply those choices to any (or all) of these four designs. You will see that in the four examples, different tones are very much in evidence, and note how these are used to impose upon the 'background space' to make this just as interesting as the subject. In 50*a*, the design is based on an unwound reel of film and its shadows. In 50*b*, the figure is an almost abstract shape devoid of detail, but her tulle overskirt provides a wonderful softening effect to the interesting outline. In 50*c*, the only highlights are seen along the sheep's back, the 'negative' gate and the top strip of sky. The darkest parts are carefully balanced around the lower body, head and legs of the sheep as well as the lower tree-line. Tones are easier to see if you look at the pictures through half-closed eyes or, if you wear spectacles, remove them! With reference to the previous embroidery (49), use only one or

51

two stitches to obtain the same effect of varying tones made by overlapping stitches, with fine lines too where these are needed.

In the photograph of the bare hedgerow in winter (51) the tones are also easy to recognize, the heavy winter sky, the pale field beyond, and the foreground of stark and prickly branches. Paint may be used on any of these examples to help cover large plain areas where no texture is needed. Use stitches which you have not tried before and choose colours carefully. You may like to try these designs in blackwork as well as in free stitchery, since the variation in tone is exactly what you would look for in a suitable design for that technique. Enlarge the designs to whatever size is most convenient.

52 *'Garden Seat', canvas work. 9.5 × 11 cm (3³/₄ × 4¹/₄ in.).*

53

One method of moving quickly into the design without having to draw or plan is shown here (52), where a very small magazine cutting becomes the centrepiece of an embroidery. The second stage is to extend the colours in stitchery (here tent stitch has been used) on to the canvas so that the picture is enlarged and extended. This is almost the reverse of (46) and (47), in which the outside area was excluded to concentrate on the design inside the square; this one takes the design *beyond* the boundaries. To do this, choose a canvas mesh in scale with the detail on the chosen photograph or painting (it might be a family group), choose the colours needed very carefully in *daylight*, as an exact match is essential, but do not stick the picture on to the canvas at this stage. On the canvas, outline the area to be covered by the picture and leave this empty while you embroider. Keep the paper picture in pristine condition while you match up the edges during work, and only stick it down on the canvas after blocking and mounting.

A small sampler of canvas work stitches, in which some textured yarns have been wrapped around strips of card and stuck between stitched rows, is shown in 53. This adds extra texture and overcomes the problem of not being able to use textured yarns on canvas unless they are couched. In cases where the stitches do not cover the canvas completely (note the lower rows) it is often necessary to work rows of back stitches over the bare threads, or to paint the canvas the same colour as the threads before work begins.

6
Counted thread: three techniques

There are many techniques which fall under the heading of 'counted thread', but three of the best known are canvas work (or, in the USA, needlepoint), blackwork and cross stitch. There is only room enough to mention them briefly here and suggest a few ways in which students of embroidery might enjoy experimenting with them.

Experiments in canvas work

Try out some of the following ideas and record them in your notebook with samples and comments.

- Use stitches other than the conventional stitches of canvas work, for example, raised chain band, chain stitch and buttonhole stitch.
- Use unusual threads, ribbons and cords, torn strips of fabric (nylon tights), string, etc.
- Use a wide variety of canvas meshes ranging from very fine to very coarse, even rug canvas, soft canvases, wire mesh and metal grids.
- Take a traditional florentine pattern and do something quite different with it – use different types of threads (some fine and some thick), or upset the balance in some way, and the direction too.
- Link canvas work with another technique as has been done in several of the illustrations in this book. Think of other ways, and experiment.

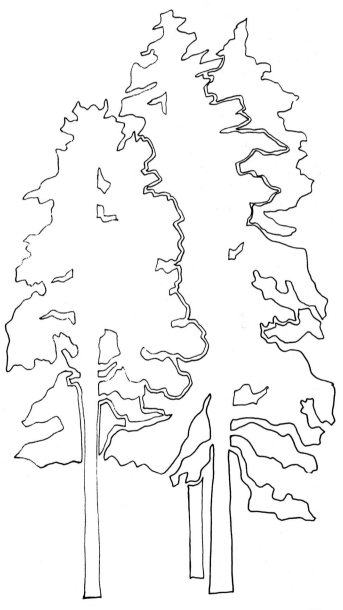

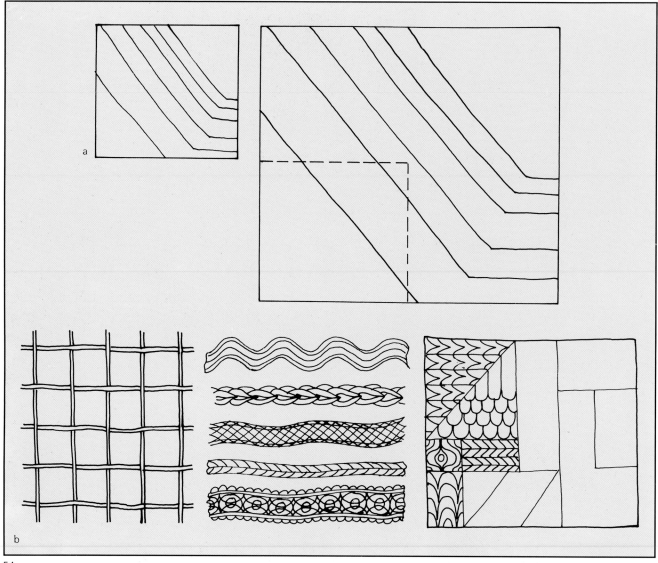

54

Project 1

This is an exercise in working to different scales on several mesh sizes, scaling up a design from the very fine (with much detail) to very coarse, with an enlarged detail of one small part. In the photograph (55) are three small embroideries, each one the same size. The top right-hand one is worked on very fine canvas in stranded cottons, and represents a tiny piece of pattern from an oriental carpet. The one next to it is the same size, but on coarser canvas, and only one quarter of the original design has been used, enlarged four times. This is worked in stranded wools and cottons. The third sample, again, is a quarter of the previous one, and a fourth one could have been made on rug canvas. The diagrams used for this exercise are shown in (54).

To work an exercise along the same lines:

1 Choose a design which has an 'all-over' pattern and translate part of this as accurately as possible on to fine canvas in fine stitches.
2 Mask three-quarters of the finished piece and copy the most interesting quarter, enlarging it to the same size as the first one.

72

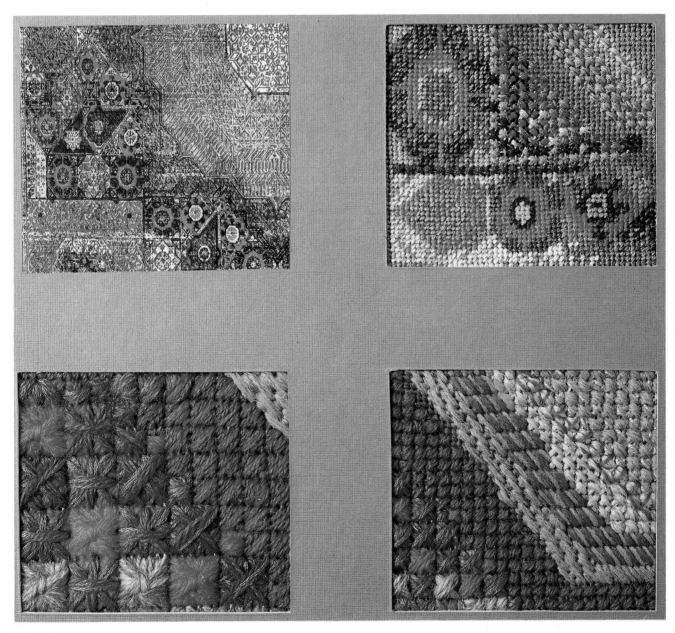

55

3 Transfer this to a coarser canvas and choose threads to match. Pretend that you are looking through a magnifying glass and use stitches which best suit the new scale of the piece.

4 Now pretend that you are looking through a microscope! Repeat **2** and **3**, but do not use the same stitches as you did for the previous ones. Remember that even the smallest dots of colour will be magnified, as will the shapes and the textures. For the fourth one, use rug canvas and thick threads, ribbon, strings, etc., and create a very highly textured surface.

5 Mount all these together on board of the same basic colour.

56 A frame for a page from the Book of Kells. 19 cm (7½ in.) square. This small embroidery is worked on soft canvas in crewel wools and stranded cottons (embroidery floss). The colours were carefully chosen to match exactly those on a page from the illuminated gospels: soft faded blues, yellows and pink/oranges on a background of old parchment. The pattern was adapted from small sections of the same page, the colours drifting and blending into each other. The figure inside the frame is a print, and the archway emphasizes its curved shape.

Blackwork

Fabrics: all types of evenweave linens and cottons, scrim, hessian, fine soft canvases or loosely woven wools. Any colours.

Threads: for experimental purposes, use any in a range of colours, though very shiny ones will probably not be as useful as the softer stranded cottons.

For this technique, we must accustom ourselves to looking for shapes of various tones (as on page 68), rather than linear designs. The stitches need a certain amount of space in which to show off their various patterns, so areas which are too small tend to break the patterns up before they become established. Therefore, the smaller the area to be covered, the smaller the stitch-pattern we must choose. The density is another factor to be assessed, and this can be decided by the stitch itself (some are 'closer' than others), by the number of extra lines we add or leave out of a basic stitch, and also by the type and thickness of the threads.

Exercise 1

1 Using only one type of yarn (do not alter the thickness of it), work a block of stitches, changing the density by missing out parts of the stitch as you go along. The effect should be noticably denser at one end than the other.
2 Using the same, or a different stitch, work in a stranded cotton first with all six strands and then gradually reducing the number until you are working with only one. Keep the stitch the same all the way through. Again, this should show a definite change in density.
3 Combine **1** and **2** to produce a greater degree of change by missing out parts of the stitch *and* by reducing the thickness of the threads.

Exercise 2

1 Choose a random-dyed thread and try some blackwork stitches with it to see how some parts of it appear and disappear. If you choose a fabric of the same colour as one of those in the thread, the area where the two same colours coincide will not show the effect of the stitches.
2 To gain a similar effect, try the idea the other way round with a plain thread on a patterned evenweave fabric. Record the results of these exercises in your notebook and keep them for reference.
3 Try blackwork stitches also on stripes, checks and spots to break up the regularity of the pattern.

Exercise 3

Make use of overlaid fabrics such as organdie, chiffon and nets to cover parts of a design and to add to the effect of gradually changing tones. Insert pieces of lace, ribbon and sequin waste among the stitches to find out what other effects can be achieved.

Exercise 4

Work blackwork stitches in conjunction with other techniques such as appliqué, canvas work, cross stitch, fabric-painting, pattern-darning and free stitchery. Try to achieve a total combination, not just two different techniques next to each other.

57

Project 2

Newspaper print is probably the nearest thing to the patterns made by blackwork stitches and so is extremely useful in the planning stage of a design when we are not sure (and find it difficult to visualize) how the areas of dark, medium and light should be arranged. Cut up some pieces of newsprint according to their density, and use them to make a collage of shapes (either on the negative or positive parts of the design), as has been done in 57. You can keep on changing these even after they have been stuck in place simply by sticking other pieces on top (parts of this design have two and three layers) and thus building up the required effect. Any dirty smudges left by glue or mistakes can be whited out with typewriter correcting fluid, or blacked in with a fibre-tip pen. This will then show you quite clearly the best places to put the stitches, especially if you look at your paper design with half-closed eyes.

This particular design is the same one used on pages 42 and 43, and could be worked (on a background of blackwork) in either appliqué, padding or free stitchery in bright colours.

58 'Poppies', a panel by Victoria Macleod. 34.5 × 47 cm (13½ × 18½ in.). Initially an experiment in screen printing, this colourful piece proved an excellent foil for coloured blackwork stitches. These were worked in a fine red thread to add a touch of intricate pattern among the strong reds and greens.

b

c

59

a

Cross stitch exercises

Although best known as a counted thread technique, cross stitch can also be used effectively as a 'free' stitch in a mixture of sizes and threads placed at random, instead of in rows. Stitches can be piled on top of each other to build up density of colours and textures, and some can be graded to the smallest size possible.

The small sample shown here (60) was worked freely in this way, allowing a much greater freedom to express the shapes and tones of the design. This originated from a magazine photograph of a wild garden (59a) which was then partly re-drawn in coloured pencils (59b). The latter was then translated literally into free cross stitch (59c) by means of different-sized stitches worked at random, beginning with the bottom layer and piling them up like layers of paint until the colours and tones looked like the pencil sketch. This kind of exercise can be worked on any

kind of fabric, not just evenweave, as the threads are not counted at any stage.

Try a similar exercise, working freely from a coloured pencil or paint sketch with a minimum of planning, so that the result resembles an impressionist painting. For ideas, look at reproductions of the Impressionists, particularly Henri-Edmund Cross, Monet and Pissarro, and aim for a similar effect of colour fusion by mixing crosses of different colours and tones together. Don't expect quick results with this exercise; it takes time to build up layers of colours and to decide where this needs to be done. Don't unpick anything either; if you don't like what you've done, keep going and use it as a base over which to add more layers of crosses. Unlike paint, the colour will not 'muddy' as you mix, but will become more textural and interesting. Use an embroidery hoop or frame to keep the fabric taut and both hands free. All kinds of fabrics and threads can be utilized, including ribbons, torn strips of fabric, knitting yarns, silks, cottons, tubular cords and string.

60 Free cross stitch experiment measuring 10 cms (4 in.) square.

Project 3

1 Take a coloured photograph which shows clearly defined areas of solid colour and try this way (61a and 61b) of planning the cross stitches on graph paper. To begin, the lines are drawn in very faintly, then the stepped lines follow them as closely as possible, after which paint or coloured pencil can be used.

2 Take a small area of the coloured graph which you have made (section off one-quarter or one-third) and then translate the colours into symbols in the manner of commercial patterns. Use crosses, lines, dots and circles for this. This exercise is for your notebook, so need not be too large, but will show the advantages of each method and may suggest ways in which both methods may be used together.

3 Traditionally, the thread used in a piece of cross stitch remains the same thickness all the way through, but let us try doing this in a different way. Try (*i*) using threads of various thicknesses; (*ii*) changing the density, size and pattern of the crosses; (*iii*) placing crosses on top of others; (*iv*) allowing the top threads to lie in different directions.

61a (*Photo: Jan Messent*)

61b

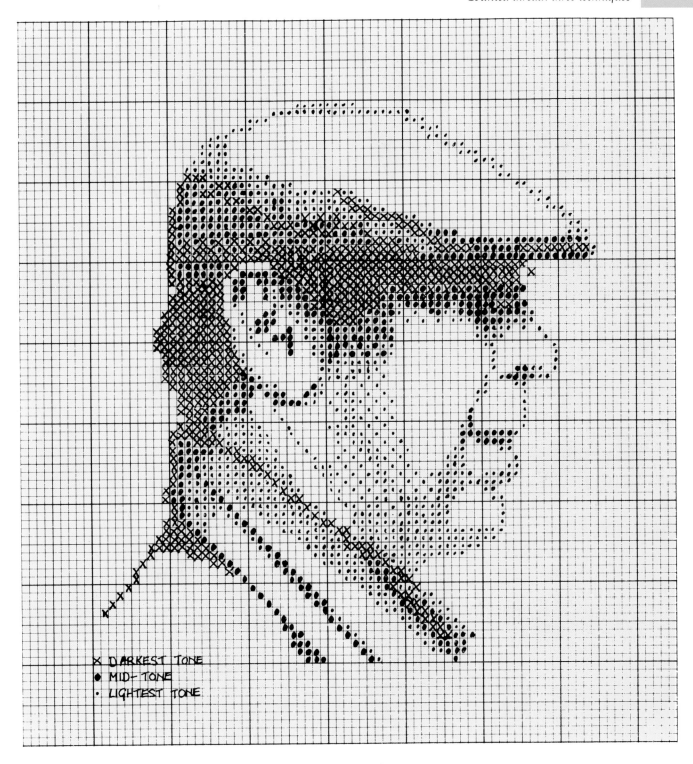

X DARKEST TONE
● MID-TONE
· LIGHTEST TONE

63 *Cross stitch window. 7.5 × 11.5 cm (3 × 4½ in.).*

64 *Pisces design in cross stitch. 7.5 × 11.5 cm (3 × 4½ in.).*

4 Spray the evenweave background fabric with paint, or use fabric crayons to vary the overall colour effect.

5 Try cross stitch on other fabrics such as hessian, canvas, scrim, binca and hardanger, and work crosses over the top of plastic vegetable nets.

6 If possible, obtain some tracing graph paper (such as the Chartwell K34G A4 pad) and lay this over a strong photograph of solid shapes, then, using symbols and outlines, mark in the main areas for a cross stitch design. This is how the chart in 62 was made, using only three symbols so that the design could be worked in tones of one colour in more or fewer strands of the same thread.

Remember that the finer the weave of the fabric, the finer the thread must be and therefore the more detail it is possible to achieve. It is most important, however, to adapt the scale of the design to the fabric and thread – or you may find that you can achieve no more detail than you could on a coarser fabric, because you have scaled the design down too much and are therefore left with a smaller version, not a more detailed one.

Remember also that if each cross is worked over two threads (as in 63 & 64), the finished embroidery will still be much smaller than it was on the graph paper, because the graph squares are bigger than your stitches. You must do some counting of threads before you begin, to make sure that you know what the finished size will be.

In both these examples, the white background is important to the design. Both were made as greetings cards, and measure about 8.5 × 12 cm (3½ × 4½ in.). They were worked in two strands of stranded cotton (embroidery floss), and in the window scene, threads of different colours have been worked over the tops of others to soften the effect of the sky and the foreground. The fishes' eyes are worked in eyelet stitch in fine gold thread, and the design represents Pisces.

7
Themes and challenges

While we may all agree that exercises and experiments are necessary, fun and educational, there are times when we need to get our teeth into something which will extend and expand our design abilities, and our knowledge of ourselves and our techniques. We can spend time dabbling in various projects and trying out different techniques, and this is useful while we are doing it, but the disquieting thought may occur to us that we are not developing along a certain line as others appear to be doing. We feel that there must be some way of doing things which is recognizably our own, and that if we had a tutor on hand to assess our work and steer us in the right direction we'd be set on the right course for the next few years. Now for those who cannot, for all kinds of reasons, attend classes where this kind of advice would be available, there is a certain amount of self-assessment which can be done, and the following suggestions are meant to be avenues along which such enquiries might lead, not necessarily in this order.

1 From the available books and publications on embroidery, or exhibitions you have seen, make notes on the techniques in which other workers appear to be specializing. Are they for example:
   • quilting: by hand, by machine, for fashion accessories, quilts, etc.;
   • machine embroidery: small panels, large hangings with appliqué, fashion embroidery, etc.?
   • three-dimensional work: on a large/small scale, fun objects, abstract, by some particular technique?
   • free stitchery: large-scale panels with appliqué, tiny miniatures, formal/traditional, pattern only, representational?
   • blackwork: formal, free-style/experimental?
2 Now make notes on their subject matter, for example:
   • landscapes;
   • architecture and houses in landscapes;
   • holiday scenes;
   • people;
   • nature/abstract;
   • nature/realistic;
   • symbolism;
   • water;
   • birds and animals;
   • flowers and plants, etc.
3 Next, make notes on the styles you can identify. Are they:
   • totally abstract, colourful or monochrome. Pattern alone?
   • impressionist, colours/techniques/ideas which portray moods and feelings, or situations?
   • precise, technically perfect, clean-cut, sharp and graphic, specific?
   • drawing (i.e. using embroidery to look like sketches)?
   • textural, often large, chunky and bold, colourful?
   • pretty, popular colours, easy on the eye, easy-to-understand subjects?
4 Make notes on the types of colours used. Are they:
   • primary colours, bold and startling?
   • pale, soft pastel colours?
   • entirely realistic?
   • 'mood' colours?
   • monochrome (goldwork comes under this heading)?
   • always analogous, or complementary, or subtle and 'meaningful'?

These four elements, techniques, subject, style and colour, are probably the most important ones which make up the personal style belonging to an embroiderer (there are other 'trace elements'). This style often enables us to be able to recognize the authorship of a piece of work without having seen it before.

To learn about your own style, make an assessment *under the same headings* of all the work you have done to date. Don't just include the bits you enjoyed, list the ones you didn't enjoy, too, as there must have been reasons which prompted you to make choices about it in the first place. *No cheating*!

Don't be surprised to find that you have more than one favourite technique, style, subject or colour. If you do, you will then have to ask yourself (i) which you enjoyed doing most, and (ii) which was the most successful.

Is there anything in all the work you have done so far which you think has more 'mileage' in it for you? In other words, is there any particular line that you began (however tentatively), which you feel you would like to explore in more depth over quite a long period of time (months or years)?

As far as colour is concerned, this is one of the most elusive and subjective elements of the four and may mean either a great deal to you, or very little. It may be a difficult element or an easy one. If there is no predominant colour in your work so far, that's all right. It simply means that you have no urge to stay with one in particular. If you find that you *do* have a dominant colour showing up in most of the things you have done, it could mean one of several things:

1 you may be in a 'colour rut', in which case you need to work on Chapter 2 for a time;
2 you may have been given a load of threads and feel that you must use them up before you acquire more! Read Chapter 2 again!
3 you may have an overriding urge to keep going in one colour-scheme for psychological reasons, known or unknown, or feel that you are able to exploit that colour-scheme to a greater degree than you have so far. These are quite valid reasons, and you should not confuse this with **1**, as the difference here is that you are *progressing*, not sticking. But just the same, read Chapter 2!

If, after making your personal list, you still feel that nothing has emerged which could give you a clue about your own leanings, then you will have to make some choices. But to leave this aside for a moment, let us suppose that some of these elements *have* appeared in a decidedly positive way, and that you have identified one or two. Whichever ones these are, therein probably lies one direction you could continue. The choices which you made were (presumably) for good reasons which suited you at the time, even if those reasons concerned economy of time, materials or effort, or your view of your own capabilities. But now you have worked on the exercises and projects in this book and you are ready for more mind-bending things. You need only a few ideas to push you forward, using your favourite technique (with some more adventurous additions), your favourite subject (more of that anon), your favourite style – which you have already discovered or must work at – and your favourite colour, which has been enriched by the exercises in Chapter 2!

If your past work has not given you any clues, your style may be dictated to a certain extent by the technique you prefer. It may also be discovered by asking yourself what kind of person you are basically and *how you would like to express yourself in embroidery*. Do not confuse this with the question, 'How do I want the world to see me through my embroidery?' unless you have first decided that you are embroidering less (i) as a means of personal expression than (ii) as a way of showing yourself to the world and/or making sales. For some, fortunate people, (i) and (ii) are the same thing, but for many, the two are not entirely compatible. Whatever conclusion you reach, do not fight against it simply because you admire what other successful embroiderers are doing and would like to emulate their styles. This can be a time-consuming occupation and will do nothing to develop your own unique abilities. Admire, but do not envy or emulate: do your *own* thing. One last thought on style. The style you adopt (or more precisely, the one which adopts *you*) for one technique may not be the same one which is used on another, since some techniques will not bend in all directions to our will! You may thoroughly enjoy doing textural and bold wall-hangings on a large scale while also finding relief in the most precise and demanding pulled-work in miniature. This is perfectly normal, and only becomes a nuisance when these diversions go in too many directions and therefore take time away from important developments.

Now to subject matter. This is such a huge topic that it needs a whole book to itself, but at least we can look at our own work so far and see whether there are any indications which may lead us to think that one topic is more apparent than any of the others. There may have been one subject in particular which you enjoyed doing and thought at the time that other ideas along the same lines were forming, if only you had the time/energy/courage to do them. Is that a line worth pursuing now? If nothing comes forward as being exciting or interesting enough, let us look at others in the hope that some word or thought will spark off an idea, and that this will generate more ideas to keep us going for a long time. Don't dismiss anything as being 'too difficult': every idea can be simplified or developed to your own requirements.

One of the most rewarding aspects of delving into a theme is the amount of fascinating research to be done, building a little knowledge into a long-term investigation and development of considerable depth. Take the subject of historic costume, for instance. The avenues to be explored are too numerous to mention, but just two of them are shown here.

Instead of taking an era, take one detail of dress: sleeve decoration, purses and bags, hair ornaments, etc. Make copious and detailed drawings of these findings, as shown

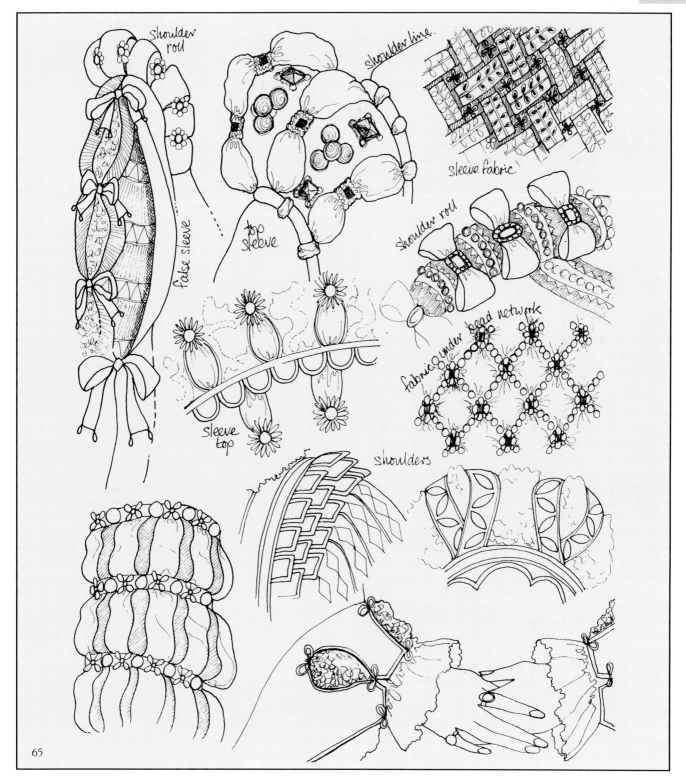

shoulder roll

shoulder line

sleeve fabric

false sleeve

top sleeve

shoulder roll

fabric under bead network

sleeve top

shoulders

65

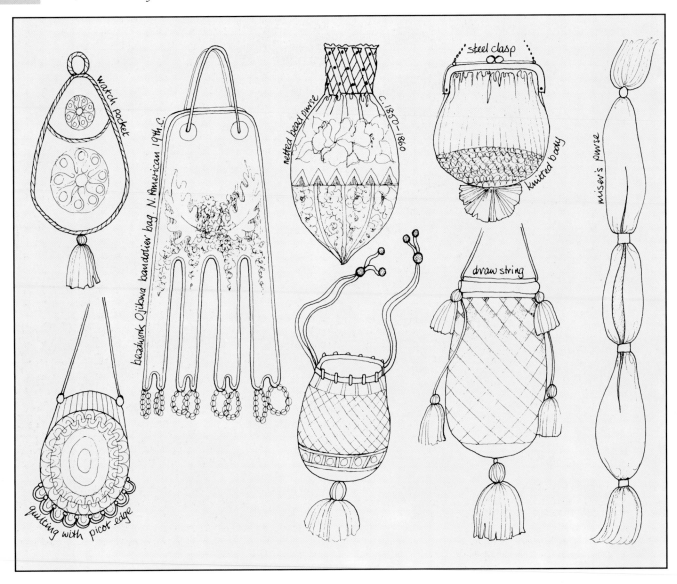

watch pocket

beadwork Ojibwa bandolier bag. N. American 19th.C.

quilting with picot edge

netted bead purse

c.1850—1860

steel clasp

knitted body

draw string

miser's purse

66

here, and then experiment to re-translate these details and constructions in a modern way, using the fabrics you have at home or can find elsewhere. All of these ideas can be tried out in our own methods of embroidery and with new up-to-date fabrics and innovations. The bags and purses are both decorative and functional and show a wealth of ideas which can be copied in a variety of techniques – imagine the miser's purse in quilted satin or shot silk or encrusted with beads. Shoes and stockings are also an interesting subject, as are hats and headgear from all ages and all countries.

67 'Metamorphic Forest', by Yvonne Morton. An abstract panel measuring 35.5 × 40.5 cm (14 × 16 in.). The fabrics used were organzas, silks and dyed background fabric. Techniques include surface stitchery, machine stitchery and beading.

The inspiration behind the design arose from a dream of a forest breaking into a line of flames, changing texture and colour and thereby undergoing a transformation in a matter of moments from a green and living thing to charred and broken stubble, grey and green ashes.

The design was worked directly from contact with the fabrics, first by working stitchery in a fairly representational way as the dream was remembered, and then by 'fragmenting' the result. This involved cutting up the embroidered fabric and rearranging the pieces to form an abstract design which more closely resembled the impression left by the dream than the moving picture which was the dream. More hand and machine embroidery was then applied to these pieces, partly to attach them to the background and partly to add more texture and impact.

68 'Air, Earth, Fire and Water', by Victoria Macleod. This small panel, 38 cm (15 in.) square, was made within strict limitations of size, for a competition, and is worked entirely in canvas embroidery. Victoria chose to use the diagonal slant of the canvas, which gives an entirely different appearance to the background of tent stitch. Use has been made of some of the more conventional canvas work stitches such as Florentine, Rhodes, Norwich, and pinwheel stitch (which appears on the white 'Air' section), but others generally associated with free stitchery have been used too – buttonhole, chain, double knot, bullion and french knots. The tiny central swirl of mixed elements is an interesting way of uniting the four sections.

8
Display and presentation

The way in which we present and display our work is of the utmost importance and goes a long way towards reflecting our own attitudes towards the work we do. I cannot stress too strongly that our involvement with a piece of embroidery (or indeed with any artwork which needs to be presented) is not finished when we have made the last stitches. The 'aftercare' should reflect its importance in the scheme of things of which it is a part, though unfortunately many very able embroiderers do not realize how their work can be ruined or improved by the method of presentation, and students who must often show their work for assessment need to be completely confident that it will be seen in the best possible light.

There are various methods of presenting work in card mounts (singly or collectively), frames of all descriptions, mounting *over* card, and so on, but only two methods are discussed here. One of them is a method widely used by embroiderers to display small pieces and collections of samples with the preliminary artwork alongside them; this is the card mount, and many examples of this can be seen in this book. The other one is an attractive method of making a soft mount without a frame, though a frame can be put on afterwards if you wish.

Essential equipment

A long, reliable perspex ruler, a sharp pencil and soft eraser.

Thick, coloured mounting card. Beware of handling this too much, as it absorbs fingermarks very easily.

A metal 'straight-edge' ruler for accurate cutting.

A strong and *very sharp* craft knife.

A cutting board. (This is *not* a luxury!)

A strong, clear PVA adhesive.

About eight large bulldog clips.

ELIZABETHAN GARDEN DESIGNS

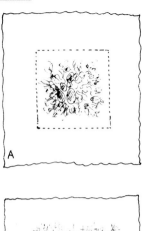

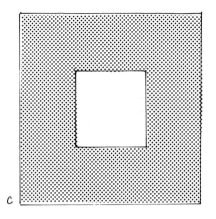

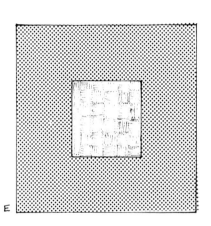

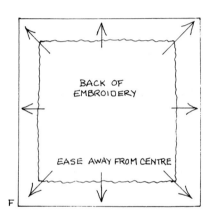

69

The window mount

1 Decide on the size of the window needed (A). Measure the embroidery and decide whether to show the background all round the design and, if so, how much. Don't crowd the design with a window which is too small. You may prefer to exclude the edges of the embroidery if these are messy (B), so decide on the trimming line. Do not cut these bits off as they will be hidden by the frame.
2 Cut the window out of the card (C), making all pencil lines *on the back*. Leave a generous border all round, and make the lower border either the same as the top and sides, or a little deeper. Do not skimp the border: a too-narrow frame looks mean and ineffective.
3 Turn the frame face downwards and glue round the edge of the window (D). Do not put glue on the embroidery, but always on the card.
4 Keeping the embroidery flat on the table, lift up the card frame and place it, glue side down, on to the embroidery, taking great care to position it exactly (E). Press down gently.
5 Now turn over both card and embroidery together, wrong side up, and ease the fabric taut with your thumbs, pulling gently away from the centre so that no wrinkles show on the right side (F). Keep checking the front to see that the position has not been disturbed before the glue dries. If necessary, use bulldog clips to hold it together until set.
6 If this is to be a single mount (as shown) cover the entire back of the card with stiff paper cut marginally smaller than the frame. Glue it carefully in position. You may have to trim the fabric a little at this stage, so that it is completely hidden by the backing. Use bulldog clips to hold this in position until dry, but take care not to mark the front.

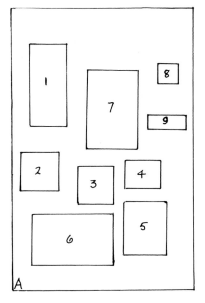

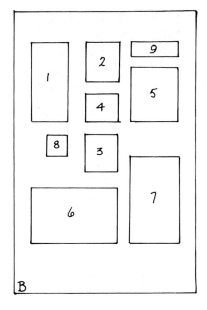

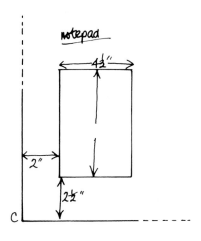

70

The collective display

This also makes use of the window mount technique described on the previous page, so what follows are useful hints on planning and presentation.

1 Paper samples (cuttings, drawings, etc.) may be *stuck* on to the board, but should be aligned in the same way as the embroideries.
2 Some unequal spaces are more interesting than having too many samples squashed up together.
3 Make sure that the two side borders are of equal widths and that the lower border is somewhat wider than the top. It is not nowadays incorrect to have these measurements equal.
4 Colour similarity in the samples creates a sense of unity; a colour which contrasts too much with the others will upset the balance.
5 The colour of the card is *critical*, and the wrong colour will do nothing to enhance the embroideries. Choose one which belongs to the same colour family (analogous) for safety, as the majority of the samples. Stone, grey, black, cream or white are safe alternatives. Silver and gold are useful, too (especially for metal thread embroidery), but try out several colours before you begin cutting.
6 The two diagrams shown here (70*a* and *b*) show a poor arrangement compared to a better one using the same pieces. 70*a* is haphazard and untidy, while 70*b* shows how the edges of shapes can be lined up with each

other on two, three or four sides to achieve a balance and feeling of organization. This is important to *any* type of display board.

7 Any labelling should be done in the same immaculate and organized manner, as this can easily spoil an otherwise perfect layout. Unless your handwriting is perfect italic script, or another beautiful and readable style, use typewritten labels. These should be either (*i*) placed all together in one block referring to the pieces by letter or number – this block should become part of the finished arrangement; or (*ii*) small individual labels stuck in exactly the same position under each one. These should be clear but unobtrusive.
8 For extra effect, each piece may first be mounted under white card, then under a slightly larger window of coloured card to show a white rim round the edge. A very *carefully positioned* line may, instead, be ruled around each window, but this requires a steady hand and eye.
9 Use a notepad (70*c*) to note all measurements. Lines are ruled on the reverse (white) side of the coloured card as shown, but remember to allow for this, or you will find that everything is the wrong way round!
10 Begin cutting from each corner. Use a *very sharp knife* on a cutting mat, and score gently first along each line before cutting through. Use the metal straight-edge ruler to guide your knife, and keep the corners clean.

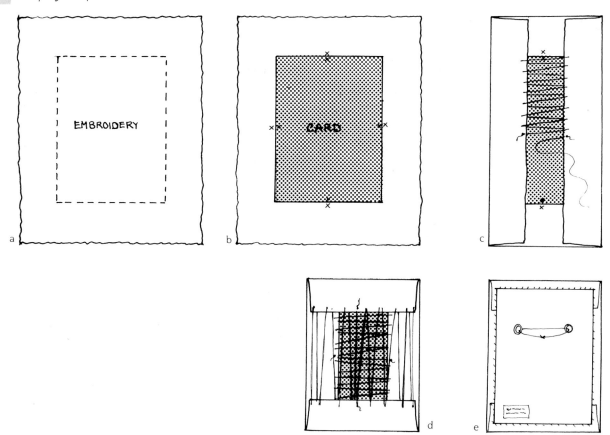

The fabric mount

This is a method for making quite a substantial mount for a piece of work, provided that the embroidery has enough spare fabric around the edge. If the fabric is loosely woven (like scrim and some evenweaves) the corners of the card or hardboard will push through, so a second layer of more closely woven fabric may be needed between the embroidery and the card.

71a shows how the area of embroidery is measured and marked with a running stitch all round.

71b The card stiffening should be exactly the same size as the marked area. Card must be very thick and stiff, or use hardboard. Bendy card will not do. Mark the exact centres of each side, both the fabric and the card.

71c Match up the centre marks, fold over the two sides and hold in place with pins while you lace across with strong thread. Begin at the centres and work outwards towards the edges. Check to see that the embroidery is still in position. Stitches should be very close together to avoid pull marks showing on the right side. Tighten the threads and secure firmly.

71d Now fold the top and bottom as shown, not allowing the flaps to show on the right side. Lace again from centres to sides with close stitches. Fold the corners down very precisely, pin in place so that no extra fabric shows on the right side, and sew down with tiny neat stitches.

71e Now cover the back completely with a piece of plain fabric, the edges of which should be folded in. This is sewn in place with invisible stitches. Rings and hanging threads can be sewn to the back, and a name-label attached at one corner.

Further reading

Colour

Constance Howard, *Embroidery and Colour*, Batsford paperback
Helen Varley (ed.), *Colour*, Marshall Editions
Kathleen Whyte, *Design in Embroidery*, Batsford

Fabrics

Valerie Campbell-Harding, *Textures in Embroidery*, Batsford paperback
Beverley Gordon, *Feltmaking*, Watson Guptill
Jean Littlejohn, *Fabrics for Embroidery*, Batsford

Stitches

Jan Beaney, *Stitches: New Approaches*, Batsford paperback
Jacqueline Enthoven, *The Stitches of Creative Embroidery*, Reinhold (USA)
Needlework School, Windward (UK, USA)
Mary Thomas, *Mary Thomas's Embroidery Book*, Hodder & Stoughton (UK), Dover Publications (USA)

Counted Thread

Jo Ippolito Christensen, *The Needlepoint Book*, Prentice Hall (USA)
Helen Fairfield, *Counted Thread Embroidery*, Batsford (UK), St Martin's Press (USA)
Elisabeth Geddes and Moyra McNeill, *Blackwork Embroidery*, Dover Publications (USA)
Needlework School (see above)
Audrey Ormrod, *Cross Stitch*, A. & C. Black (UK), Wallace Homestead Book Company (USA)
Sarah Windrum, *Needlepoint*, Octopus

Useful addresses

UK

The following people supply materials for the embroiderer by mail order, though some only run a postal service (so you need to know beforehand more or less exactly what you require). In any case, it is always a good idea to send a large stamped addressed envelope to ask for information about their system and supplies. Some charge a small fee for their samples.

England

Avon

Magpie's Embroidery Centre
Broad Street Place
Broad Street
Bath
Avon
(0225 526622)

Buckinghamshire

'Shades' (Sheila Read)
57 Candlemas Lane
Beaconsfield
Buckinghamshire HP9 1AE
(04946 2956)
(hard to find items)

Cheshire

Hepatica
82A Water Lane
Wilmslow
Cheshire
(0625 526622)

Silken Strands
33 Linksway
Gatley
Cheadle
Cheshire SK8 4LA
(061 4289108)

Cleveland

Beldale Crafts
121 Raby Road
Hartlepool
Cleveland TS24 8DT
(0429 221972)

Leven Crafts
23 Chaloner Street
Guisborough
Cleveland TS14 6QD
(0287 39177)

Cornwall

Vivien Prideaux
Mile Hill
Porthtowan
Truro
Cornwall TR4 8TY
(0202 890252)

Derbyshire

Mary Allen
Wirksworth
Derbyshire DE4 4BN
(062 982 2504)

Essex

In Stitches
48 Kings Road
Brentwood
Essex CM14 4DW
(0277 230448)

Gloucestershire

Cotswold Craft Centre
Dept E
5 Whitehall
Stroud
Gloucestershire GL5 1HA
(Stroud 2220)

Hampshire

Pauline Deverell
'Mylor'
Church Hill
West End
Southampton
Hampshire S03 3AT
(0703 473400)

Lancashire

Threadbare
5 Forester Drive
Fence
Burnley
Lancashire BB12 9PG
(0282 601069)

London

(embroidery tuition)
'Stitch Design'
Textile Art School and Gallery
120 Cannon Workshops
West India Dock
Isle of Dogs
London E14
(01-987 2835)

Excellent embroidery courses by post. Write for details to Julia Caprara.

Merseyside

The Sewing Basket
4 Chapel Alley
Formby
Liverpool L37
(07048 70451)

Telephone/mail order service.

Voirrey Embroidery
18 Hilary Drive
Upton
Wirral
Merseyside L49 6LD
(051 677 7393)

Twenty-four-hour answering service.

Norfolk

The Handworker's Market
The Shire Hall
Shirehall Plain
Holt
Norfolk NR25 6BG

Northumberland

The Calico Tree
6 Alemouth Road
Hexham
Northumberland NE46 3PJ
(0434 602065)

Somerset

Audrey Babington's *Workbox*
   (send 24p stamp)
40 Silver Street
Wiveliscombe
Somerset TA4 2NY

Warwickshire

The Nimble Thimble
26 The Green
Bilton
Rugby
Warwickshire
(0788 817911)

Wiltshire

Mace and Nairn
89 Crane Street
Salisbury
Wiltshire

Yorkshire

Highthorn Embroidery
Beadlam
Nawton
Yorks
(0439 71278)

Spinning Jenny
Market Place
Masham
nr Ripon
North Yorks HG4 4EB
(0765 89351)

Spinning Jenny
Bradley
Keighley
West Yorks BD20 9DD
(0535 32469)

Scotland

The Embroidery Shop
51 William Street
Edinburgh EH3 7LW
(031 225 8642)

Needlecraft
201 King Street
Castle Douglas
Kirkcudbright DG7 1DT
(0556 3606)

Christine Riley
53 Barclay Street
Stonehaven
Kincardineshire
Scotland AB3 2AR
(0569 63238)

The Textile Workshop and Gallery
Gladstone's Land
Lawnmarket
Edinburgh EH1 2NT
(031 225 4570)

Wales

'Something Special'
105 Meliden Road
Prestatyn
Clwyd LL19 8LU
(074 56 88162 *and* 4127)

Brodwaith Embroidery
Queens Square
Dolgellau LL40 1AN
(0341 422325)

Richmond Art and Craft
Dept E1
181 City Road
Cardiff CF2 3JB
(0222 490119)

Tri Thy Craft Centre
Coed Talon
Mold
Clwyd CH7 4TU
(0352 771359)

USA

Chain stores which usually stock a
good selection of embroidery
needs:

Ben Franklin Stores
Jefferson Stores

Kay Mart
M.H. Lamston
The May Co.
Neisners
J.C. Penney Stores
Sears Roebuck
Two Guys
Woolworths

Embroidery supplies mail order:

The Hidden Village
215 Yale Avenue
Claremont
California 91711

Lew Wards
Elgin
Illinois 60120

Peters Valley Craftsmen
Layton
New Jersey 07851

Economy Handicrafts
50-21 69th Street
Woodside
New York 11377

The Counting House at the
    Hammock Shop
Box 155
Pawleys Island
South Carolina 29585

American Handicrafts
2617 W Seventh Street
Forth Worth
Texas 76707

Canada

Thistledown
102A Main Street
P.O. Box 114
Picton
Ontario KOK 2TO

Embroiderers' Guild Addresses

UK

The Embroiderers' Guild
Apartment 41
Hampton Court Palace
East Molesey
Surrey KT6 9AU

USA

The Embroiderers' Guild of America
200 Fourth Avenue
Louisville
Kentucky 40202

Australia

The Embroiderers' Guild of
    Australia
175 Elizabeth Street
Sydney
New South Wales 2000

Embroiderers' Guild of Victoria
170 Wattletree Road
Malvern
Victoria 3144

New Zealand

Association of New Zealand
    Embroiderers' Guild
171 The Ridgeway
Mornington
Wellington 2

Canada

Canadian Embroiderers' Guild
PO Box 541
Station B
London
Ontario N6A 4 W1

Index